CUSTOMER AND MARKET-DRIVEN QUALITY MANAGEMENT

Also available from ASQC Quality Press

Creating a Customer-Centered Culture: Leadership in Quality, Innovation, and Speed
Robin L. Lawton

At the Service Quality Frontier
Mary M. LoSardo and Norma M. Rossi

Quality Service Pays
Henry L. Lefevre

Deming's 14 Points Applied to Services
A. C. Rosander

Quality Service—Pure and Simple
Ronald W. Butterfield

The Customer Is King!
R. Lee Harris

To request a complimentary catalog of publications, call 800-248-1946.

CUSTOMER AND MARKET-DRIVEN QUALITY MANAGEMENT

Johnson A. Edosomwan

ASQC Quality Press
Milwaukee, Wisconsin

Customer and Market-Driven Quality Management
Johnson A. Edosomwan

Library of Congress Cataloging-in-Publication Data

Edosomwan, Johnson Aimie
    Customer and market-driven quality management / Johnson A.
    Edosomwan.
        p.   cm.
    Includes bibliographical references and index.
    ISBN 0-87389-137-6
    1. Total quality management.   2. Industrial management.
    3. Consumer satisfaction.   I. Title.
    HD62.15.E36   1993
    658.5'62 — dc20   93-5513
                                                                CIP

10 9 8 7 6 5 4 3 2 1

ISBN 0-87389-137-6

Acquisitions Editor: Susan Westergard
Production Editor: Annette Wall
Marketing Administrator: Mark Olson
Set in Janson Text by Linda J. Shepherd.
Cover design by Montgomery Media, Inc.
Printed and bound by BookCrafters, Inc.

ASQC Mission: To facilitate continuous improvement and increase customer satisfaction by identifying, communicating, and promoting the use of quality principles, concepts, and technologies; and thereby be recognized throughout the world as the leading authority on, and champion for, quality.

For a free copy of the ASQC Quality Press Publications Catalog, including ASQC membership information, call 800-248-1946.

Printed in the United States of America

   Printed on acid-free recycled paper

  ASQC
                     Quality Press
                     611 East Wisconsin Avenue
                     Milwaukee, Wisconsin 53202

This book is dedicated
to my
family and friends.

Contents

Acknowledgments

Many people contributed to the successful completion of this book. My thanks and love is expressed to my wife, Mary, and children, Esosa, Efe, and Johnson Jr., for their support and encouragement. I am grateful for the assistance and support of the staffs of Johnson & Johnson Associates, Inc. and ASQC Quality Press. During the preparation of this book, I experienced several difficulties and obstacles that were overcome through the grace of God. I am grateful for the guidance and wisdom received from God during the preparation of this book.

Introduction

This book was written to help enterprises with new technologies and tools become market driven through improvement in product and service quality, productivity, and total customer satisfaction. Trends show that production and service enterprises continue to need new approaches to respond to four major challenges. First, changes in the political, economic, and regulatory environments have significantly increased competition in all industrial sectors. This problem is compounded with the new consumer-oriented market revolution that demands excellent quality products and services at competitive prices.

Second, unpredictable slowdown in overall market growth poses the problem of too much capacity chasing too few buyers. This problem is compounded by new technological, economic, and social forces in the marketplace which collectively reduce or eliminate the life cycles of new products and services. The third challenge involves the design of effective and efficient organizational structures and management systems that permit continuous process improvement through innovative problem solving and error-prevention philosophy. A key factor in facing this challenge is providing the required new knowledge, innovative processes, and tools to managers and employees to improve quality and productivity at the source of production and service.

The fourth and final challenge involves developing a customer-oriented culture where people are highly motivated to work and grow in a productive total quality culture that is integrated and highly participative. Integral to the success in meeting this challenge is enhancing partnership and teamwork between suppliers, process owners, and customers while improving competitive posture through increased market share, profitability, and growth. This book was written to address these challenges and help enterprises with practical ways to implement new quality and productivity technologies to achieve total customer satisfaction and competitiveness.

This is the first book that focuses on how to integrate market-driven concepts, marketing aspects of quality, statistics, productivity, human resource and change management, and customer focus in one package. The book provides essential techniques, technologies, tools, methodologies, framework, and principles for resolving product and service quality problems and improving productivity and total customer satisfaction at the operational unit and enterprise levels.

The book evolved out of several years of research, teaching, consulting, and industrial work experience in the areas of quality, productivity, and total customer satisfaction management. The book also includes materials from seminars and workshops conducted nationally and internationally. The methodologies and case studies are taken from real-life experiences in both manufacturing and service organizations.

This book was written with the belief that achieving total customer satisfaction requires an understanding of market needs and requirements, marketing aspects of quality, statistics, teamwork, and problem-solving techniques for total quality improvement, as well as commitment from management and employees to do the job right the first time at the source of production and service. This book also follows the premise that an integrated systems approach to problem solving is required for improvement in quality, productivity, and total customer satisfaction.

This book is organized into ten chapters and five appendices. Chapter 1 provides the description and definitions of a market-driven and customer-oriented enterprise. Practical steps and approaches are provided on the requirements of becoming a market-driven and customer-oriented enterprise. Market-driven focus elements and the success factors for becoming a successful market-driven enterprise are discussed. Chapter 2 provides the methodologies, tools, and techniques for implementing total quality management (TQM) and the continuous improvement philosophy for all work processes. It includes a step-by-step approach on how to create partnership with the customer, as well as continuous improvement guidelines. Chapter 3 discusses techniques for total customer satisfaction management; presents a customer satisfaction model; and provides practical steps to improve customer satisfaction, enhance customer-supplier-process-owner partnership, and track customer satisfaction levels. Chapter 4 outlines a step-by-step approach for problem solving and completed staff work; presents tools and techniques for total quality and productivity management; and presents guidelines and mechanisms to facilitate group and individual problem solving.

Chapter 5 discusses specific techniques for error prevention and presents the quality error-prevention model. Emphasis is placed on a step-by-step process for preventing quality errors at the source of production and service. The methodology for implementing the quality error removal technique is provided, and various types of quality costs are discussed. Chapter 6 covers the sources of variation in production and service work environments and gives strategies for controlling variation. In Chapter 7, the sigma approach to TQM is discussed with a step-by-step approach for implementing the concept. Also, techniques and tools for process management and control are provided.

Chapter 8 presents a framework for developing market-driven leaders, managers, and professionals. Ideas for improving managerial performance and implementing effective training programs are discussed. This chapter also discusses how to achieve excellence through people, teamwork, and participative management, and provides steps for correcting poor performance and improving individual productivity. Chapter 9 focuses on how to implement quality and productivity improvement projects. The 9C principles for project management, and process-oriented principles for project management and process-oriented improvement ideas are presented. Strategies for managing change and overcoming common implementation problems are also discussed. In Chapter 10 a summary of key success factors and recommended action items is provided to assist enterprises interested in becoming market driven and implementing continuous improvement in quality, productivity, and total customer satisfaction. The appendices provide case studies, statistical tables, suggested references for further reading, checklists, and sources for obtaining additional information on computer programs for quality management.

How to Use This Book

This book is action oriented in content and style. It therefore provides step-by-step guidelines, tools, and techniques that will return expected results when implemented. Key concepts are described to provide an understanding of the elements of successful implementation of market-driven quality. Case studies are provided in Appendix A for real-world orientation and examples of usage of the tools and techniques. A summary matrix is provided in the introduction of this book; review it and use it as a reference to select models, tools, and techniques for implementing improvement projects. Finally, this book is only meaningful when its concepts, tools, and techniques are put into practice to achieve results. Readers are encouraged to use the technologies presented in this book to ensure result-oriented continuous improvement programs.

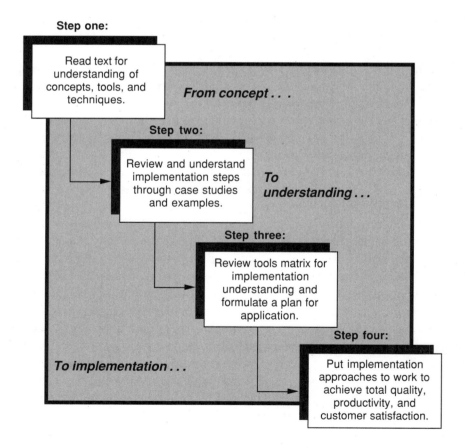

Figure I.1: How to Use This Book

Potential application areas for continuous improvement tools and techniques				
Tools/techniques	**Potential application areas**	**Level of application**		
		Individual task	Group dept.	Company
Nominal group technique	• Solving problems • Generating ideas • Managing consensus • Reducing conflict	X	X	X
Force field analysis	• Analyzing goals • Evaluating strategies for success • Moving from old to new methods and products	X	X	X
Cause-and-effect diagram	• Solving problems • Assessing root cause(s) of problems • Assessing impact of potential causes • Using logic reassuring tool	X	X	X
Edosomwan error mapping technique	• Eliminating defects • Removing errors • Improving quality, productivity, and performance	X	X	
Edosomwan quality error prevention model	• Establishing framework for quality improvement • Eliminating defects and errors	X	X	
Quality error removal technique	• Solving problems by action team • Improving total quality • Using team error prevention	X	X	
Production and service improvement technique (PASIT)	• Eliminating non–value-added waste • Improving processes • Improving productivity and quality	X	X	
Productivity and quality assessment matrix (PAQAM)	• Balancing productivity and quality requirements • Managing performance	X	X	X
Market-driven model	• Formulating steps to become a market-driven enterprise • Satisfying market requirements • Creating a customer-oriented culture		X	X
Market analysis model (MAM)	• Understanding customer preferences • Using market analysis and segmentation		X	X
PEAD model	• Understanding customer requirements • Defining product and service characteristics • Managing new product introduction	X	X	X
Quality function deployment	• Listening to the voice of the customer • Understanding customer requirements • Balancing requirements with product and process characteristics	X	X	X
Control charts	• Understanding process variability • Reducing product defect levels	X	X	
Problem-solving steps	• Resolving complex problems • Guiding group problem-solving efforts • Managing projects	X	X	
Change management model	• Managing total quality culture changes • Overcoming resistance to change	X	X	X

Figure I.2: How to Apply Continuous Improvement Tools and Techniques

This book is meant to serve the practical needs of four types of readers.

- Line executives and practicing managers who are responsible for quality, productivity, and customer satisfaction in organizations
- Educators and consultants for continuous improvement of work processes and TQM
- Students in engineering and business schools who need orientation on market-driven quality, productivity, and customer satisfaction management
- Process owners who make continuous improvement of work processes happen

This book will also serve as an excellent reference for seminars and workshops, as a classroom text, and as a handbook for quality, productivity, and total customer satisfaction issues.

CHAPTER 1

Becoming a Customer- and Market-Driven Enterprise

The sole purpose of a customer- and market-driven enterprise is to be profitable by satisfying customers through competitive and excellent quality products and services, and by focusing on continuous improvement of all work processes.

A customer- and market-driven enterprise is one that is committed to providing excellent quality and competitive products and services to satisfy the needs and wants of customers in a well-defined market segment. Such an enterprise has a strong customer orientation. The differences between a traditional enterprise and a customer- and market-driven enterprise are shown in Table 1.1. The customer- and market-driven enterprise analyzes its market capabilities and provides products and services to satisfy market needs. It considers its customers as the final judges who determine product and service satisfaction level, delivery, price, and performance.

In the quest for excellence in product and service leadership in a competitive world economy, enterprises must embrace the customer- and market-driven philosophy as a competitive strategy and as a means for survival. The marketplace is finite, and in a free enterprise system, there is the element of competition. Enterprises competing in the marketplace constantly evaluate the available goods and services to determine the wisest, most valuable exchange to make. The enterprise that adopts the customer- and market-driven philosophy is best able to compete in

1

Table 1.1: Traditional Organizations vs. Customer-Driven Organizations

	Traditional organizations	Customer-driven organizations
Product and service planning	• Short-term focus • Reactionary management • Management by objectives	• Long-term focus • Prevention-based management • Customer-driven strategic planning process
Measures of performance	• Bottom-line financial results • Quick returns on investment	• Customer satisfaction • Market share • Long-term profitability • Quality orientation • Total productivity
Attitudes toward customers	• Customers are irrational and a pain. • Customers are a bottleneck to profitability.	• Voice of the customer is important. • Professional treatment and attention to customers are required.
Quality of products and services	• Provided according to organizational requirements	• Provided according to customer requirements and needs
Marketing focus	• Seller's market • Careless about lost customers	• Increased market share and financial growth achieved through customer satisfaction.
Process management approach	• Focus on error and defect detection	• Focus on error and defect prevention
Product and service delivery attitude	• It is OK for customers to wait for products and services.	• It is best to provide fast-time-to-market products and services.
People orientation	• People are the source of problems and are burdens on the organization.	• People are an organization's greatest resource.
Basis for decision making	• Product-driven • Management by opinion	• Customer-driven • Management by data
Attitudes toward customers	• Hostile and careless • "Take it or leave it" attitude	• Courteous and responsive • Empathic and respectful attitude
Improvement strategy	• Crisis management • Management by fear and intimidation	• Continuous process improvement • Total process management
Mode of operation	• Career-driven and independent work • Customers, suppliers, and process owners have nothing in common.	• Management-supported improvement • Teamwork between suppliers, process owners, and customers practiced.

the marketplace by focusing on the customer-oriented management concept. Such an enterprise uses a disciplined approach to product and service management and continuous process improvement, quality as a driver, people participation, performance and productivity improvement, and total customer satisfaction. Any enterprise that is not in touch with the marketplace or customer base to understand changing needs, wants, and desires will have difficulty retaining and gaining market share. As competitors enter the market, the enterprise that is best able to anticipate market needs, translate them into products and services, and market them at an affordable price will capture a greater percentage of the market share. Such enterprises will always be rewarded with better profit margins, repeat purchases, and increasing growth.

Steps to Becoming a Customer- and Market-Driven Enterprise

The recommended steps to becoming a customer- and market-driven enterprise are shown in Figure 1.1.

Step one: Convince top management of customer- and market-driven needs and benefits. Do a thorough analysis of the market requirements. Use competitive data on products and services, market share, cost profile, and profitability to convince top management. Explain the role of the customer, quality, and productivity in organizational survival. The use of successful and unsuccessful customer- and market-driven quality examples from other companies also provides a quick way of helping executives see the benefits of adopting the customer- and market-driven philosophy. The message to top management is that improvement of quality, productivity, and performance are key to achieving competitive advantage, profitability, and growth.

Step two: Communicate the customer- and market-driven philosophy to the entire organization. Once senior management support has been achieved, the next step is to communicate and demonstrate management's commitment to customer-oriented thinking. The philosophy to be communicated should emphasize that marketing orientation begins with the customer; that is, the sole purpose of the business is to attract, serve, and satisfy customers at a profit. Satisfying market requirements is required at all levels of the organizations. Everyone should also take the responsibility for defining internal and external customers. The commitment to productivity and quality excellence means that a total

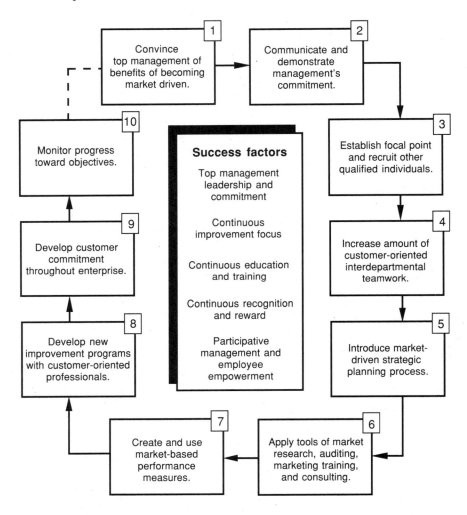

Figure 1.1: Steps to Becoming a Customer- and Market-Driven Enterprise

quality culture exists in which everyone constantly considers the quality of their work and how it is reflected in the final output. This also requires that workers be given control, responsibility, and decision latitude for a variety of activities, such as maintenance, information control, quality, process analysis, service, production, and resource allocation. Adopting a customer- and market-driven philosophy also means focusing on management with facts and customer data, quality first, proper planning, and effective utilization of human resources. Under the new philosophy, the objectives of total customer satisfaction, increase in market share, and profitability determine the enterprise's strategy.

Step three: Establish a formal market-driven and customer-oriented focal point within the enterprise. Recruit seasoned and talented individuals to develop customer-oriented improvement programs. The enterprise improvement team should benchmark successful customer- and market-driven quality practices implemented in other organizations to avoid potential sources of failure. Individuals charged with this program development must also be given the authority and resources required to institute the program elements.

Step four: Take immediate action to increase the amount of customer-oriented interdepartmental teamwork, individual productivity, and team focus on continuous improvement of work processes. People should be trained to work together toward common productivity and quality goals while sharing ownership of the final work output. Individuals and work teams should be encouraged to participate in group problem solving, decision making, and incentive systems for rewarding quality excellence. Organizational barriers that hinder teamwork should be eliminated. The method of working should focus on cooperation, not on contention. Everyone can make a difference in the quest for total quality improvement. Both management and employees should be encouraged to take greater responsibility for their work processes and to provide ideas for improving the total process. Managers and supervisors should use a participative management approach to encourage innovative ideas from everyone and to put them to work. The environment should allow managers and employees to share in decision making and problem solving and recognition, which are essential for error prevention and innovative improvements.

Step five: Introduce a customer- and market-driven strategic planning process and integrate market and customer focus into it. The enterprise's market-driven quality, productivity, and customer satisfaction strategy should describe the framework, approaches, goals, and objectives that the enterprise will follow to achieve continuous performance improvement. At every level of the enterprise, it is important to have a quality strategy consistent with customer requirements, market demands, operating principles, procedures, and policies. The quality strategy should be the responsibility of the senior management team. Senior management in each operational unit would work with its team to define tactical and operational quality strategies. The quality strategy should address quality planning, measurement, evaluation, and improvement management.

Continuous quality planning involves defining the specific strategies for understanding the market and maintaining an awareness of customer needs, wants, and desires. The plan should define opportunities for supplier and customer involvement in formulating the quality improvement element of the strategy. Based on the understanding of customer needs, the quality improvement strategy should be developed. This element of the strategy will define the process for continuous improvement and people involvement. It should recognize and support the need for new techniques, tools, procedures, and methodologies to implement improvement. Other requirements which may be included in the strategy include updated product specifications such as those for hardware and software; equipment for enhanced measurement, inspection, and testing; process control; and resource management tools.

The quality management element should define the strategy for developing the skills and knowledge required by management and employees to do the job right the first time. Plans for education and training should include technical and managerial courses, seminars, and workshops. This element should define communication channels for quality and customer awareness throughout the enterprise. Such channels of communication should ensure that customers, suppliers, employees, and stockholders are informed about quality goals, objectives, policy, direction, guidance, and performance. The quality management plan should also define specific direction and procedures for monitoring compliance to the enterprise's quality policy, ensuring successful implementation of the quality goals and objectives.

Once developed, the integrated master quality strategy for the enterprise should be reviewed and revised annually by the enterprise's quality management committee. This committee should comprise representatives from all the functional areas of the business development, manufacturing, marketing, services, and support groups. Once developed, the quality plan should be communicated to everyone with specific milestones and measurements for assessing performance.

Step six: Perform marketing research, marketing, auditing, marketing training, and marketing consulting to improve marketing practice in the enterprise. Identify the products and services to be provided; define the process sources of variation; and define non–value-added steps and ongoing focus on process measurement, evaluation, control, and improvement.

Step seven: Create and use market-based measures of performance at all levels of the enterprise. The measures should apply to managers and nonmanagers as well as to suppliers and process owners. One of the essential elements of developing a customer-oriented enterprise is deciding how the performance of managers and nonmanagers is evaluated and rewarded. Performance measurements should be more than sales volume, short-term profitability, and rate of return on investment. The focus in developing performance measures for both managers and nonmanagers should include but not be limited to the following areas: short- and long-term profits, customer satisfaction indices, quality and productivity improvement indicators, organizational development, market share indicators, human resource development, teamwork, cost management profile, rate of return on investment, and product reliability measures. Impediments to successful management of information and measures of performance include poor channels of communication and inadequate data collection processes. Communication channels such as meetings and electronic data exchange are recommended at all levels of the enterprise.

Step eight: Continually develop new improvement programs and eliminate outdated existing ones. Develop strong customer-oriented marketing professionals to support the program. The new improvement project must provide defect-free output that satisfies customer requirements. The program should encourage broad ownership and total participation by everyone, as well as accountability for results. The commitment from everyone should also include willingness to change unproductive work habits and adopt the attitude of doing the job right the first time. To achieve expected quality results, individuals and work teams should be provided with the right training and education. Quality education is essential because it prepares everyone to perform well by providing the knowledge needed to make logical, intelligent decisions. If the right skills are provided, people attain efficient work habits and positive work ethics and attitudes that lead to quality excellence. Training should focus on basic orientation to quality, techniques and tools for quality improvement, quality leadership, technical skills, process involvement, and teamwork.

Step nine: Continually develop customer commitment throughout the enterprise. Publicize successful pilot projects. Reward heroes and steady performing individuals who have made a difference. A management system that recognizes and encourages ongoing quality improvement efforts must be developed and implemented. In rewarding quality success, place emphasis on accomplishments of teams as well as individuals. Provide recognition and reward in a timely manner. Promotions, pay increases, awards, additional responsibilities, and thanks for a job well done should recognize the accomplishments of teams and individuals.

Step ten: Monitor progress toward market-oriented goals and replan accordingly. Continue to build small bricks of success in enhancing value and excellence and spreading the success throughout the enterprise.

Focus Elements of a Customer- and Market-Driven Enterprise

Once a decision is made that an enterprise will become customer- and market-driven, a clear direction and purpose must be articulated. The enterprise must focus on 11 key elements, as shown in Figure 1.2, as the basis for decision making throughout the enterprise.

Commitment to Customer Satisfaction

The first and most important element is commitment to total customer satisfaction as the foundation of the enterprise. A customer- and market-driven enterprise should be committed to focusing on customer needs, wants, and desires. The business' purpose is to attract, serve, and satisfy customers at a profit and to be the best in every market it chooses to serve. To meet this challenge, customer-oriented strategic, tactical, and operational product and service plans are developed to compete against the toughest competitors. The enterprise should also be committed to continuous partnership with customers and suppliers. This involves working with both to determine how to use new products to improve quality and productivity, and sharing a commitment to providing defect-free products, parts, and high-quality services.

Human Resource Development

The customer- and market-driven enterprise must also be committed to investing in the development of the human resource. It must treat people as its most valuable resource. This involves education to make customer

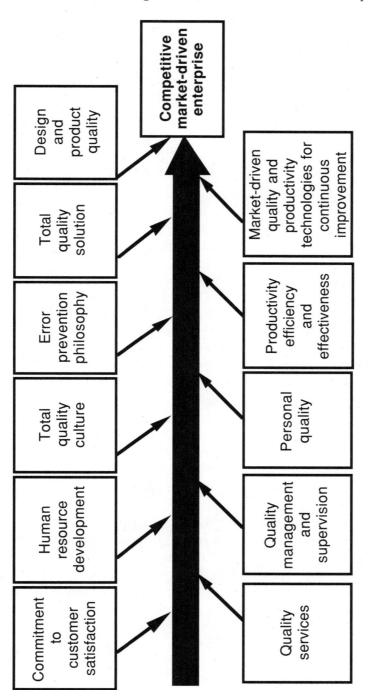

Figure 1.2: Focus Elements of a Customer- and Market-Driven Enterprise

satisfaction and quality every employee's concern. The actions of the enterprise should show its commitment to respect for the individual customer who buys and uses its products and services. This encourages employees to handle customer requests with empathy, courtesy, and satisfactory responses. The commitment also involves respect for all employees' needs for development, well-being, economic security, and the quality of working life.

Focus on Creating a Total Quality Culture

Quality improvement has been espoused as a key feature of the customer- and market-driven enterprise. This is because the relationship between customer satisfaction and quality has grown much closer over the past decade. Customers are less tolerant of poor quality. Competition has made it increasingly necessary to distinguish an enterprise's products and services on the basis of overall quality as well as price and delivery. It is no longer enough to provide the customer a desired product or service at low cost. The product or service must be delivered on time and must meet or exceed all performance requirements. Performance specifications have broadened to include ease of use and repair and mean time between failure, in addition to operational characteristics and features. Meeting customer expectations of quality, therefore, has become the hallmark of being customer driven. Fortunately, the quality culture is completely complementary to the customer-oriented culture and is equally important. When positioning an enterprise to meet or exceed customer requirements, half of the battle toward establishing a total quality culture can be won.

As with developing a customer orientation, achieving superior quality begins with developing a new culture and a revised set of values, and then disseminating these values throughout the enterprise. The total quality culture is one in which everyone in an enterprise or operational work unit constantly considers the quality of their work and how it is reflected in products and services provided to the customer. It is easy to detect the presence of a total quality culture: the company's operational policy, procedures, and processes of the enterprise reflect an obsession with quality. Figure 1.3 shows the elements of a total quality culture. Creating a total quality culture does not happen overnight; it can take several years. The process requires ongoing effort and teamwork between all functional areas of the enterprise. The process of creating a total quality culture

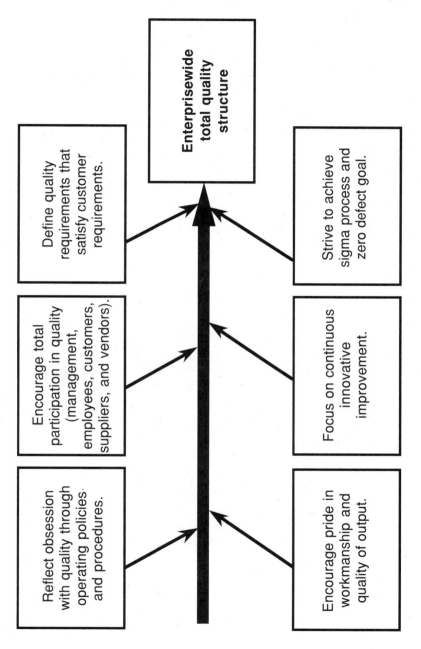

Figure 1.3: Elements of a Total Quality Culture

begins with the development of the operating policy, procedures, and processes of the enterprise to reflect an obsession with quality.

In a total quality culture, everyone has a clear understanding of the importance of quality in achieving overall business objectives. People at every level are aware of the requirements and needs of the customer. Everyone takes pride in their own work and realizes how it affects the final output of the enterprise as a whole. Top managers, customers, suppliers, and employees are encouraged to set and meet aggressive quality goals and objectives. The eventual goal is defect-free product and services. The structure of the enterprise should allow for continuous improvement. People at every level should be encouraged to innovate and to use new tools and techniques to achieve quality excellence. This will lead to total customer satisfaction in the services provided to the customer.

In addition to the emphasis on quality, the customer must become the ultimate evaluator of quality. Internal and external customer requirements must be integrated into enterprise business plans. Customer-based performance measures must be defined. A strong communication link must be developed with internal and external customers. The total quality culture emphasizes customer-oriented values and beliefs supported by the entire organization and encourages commitment throughout the enterprise's work units. The relationship between the two cultures, customer oriented and quality oriented, should be clear. The customer is the ultimate evaluator of quality, and quality is the key discriminator for the customer. An enterprise that is dedicated to integrating both aspects into its culture will be well positioned.

Top management support and leadership is required for the transition to the total quality culture. Elements for top management to focus on are shown in Figure 1.4. Top management must make a physical, mental, and philosophical commitment to quality and total customer satisfaction. This type of commitment is generally prompted by an awareness and acceptance of the need for change. If there is no strong commitment from top management, priorities will shift before results can be achieved.

Commitment is shown through ongoing support of quality and customer satisfaction improvement projects. Top management must monitor, encourage, and reward those who actively improve products, services, and processes. Commitment also involves allocating resources to correct common causes in the system that are responsible for poor quality. When long-standing systemic issues are identified and require

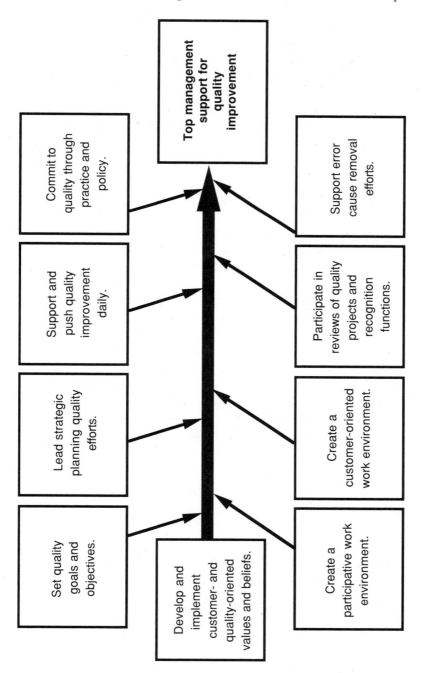

Figure 1.4: Top Management's Role in Total Quality Management

resources to be redirected for resolution, management must respond. It is also important to set specific goals and objectives to direct employee efforts. Employees must understand how their efforts support the company's strategic plan, and they must be held accountable for performance and contributions.

Top management must also be committed to utilizing statistics, measurement techniques, and data collection to control variability in human, mechanized, and automated performance. This represents a philosophical commitment that is key to success. The top management team must continue to grow, develop, and change as the culture changes. The growth involves studying, understanding, and positively directing human behavior toward excellent performance.

Responsibility for managing the economics surrounding the business remains with top management. Costs and prices must be kept at levels that allow affordable products and services to be delivered while the company remains profitable.

Two key commitments that must be continually reinforced and demonstrated by top management are to minimizing delay time, idle time, wasted time, and lost time, and to utilizing methods, procedures, and processes to ensure that the products and services rendered are of exceptional quality. Also, top management must be committed to authorizing employees to take corrective action for prevention of errors, defects, and delays at every level of the organization.

The continuous improvement philosophy must be an integral part of top management's vision, practice, and personal mission. Organizations that have a top management zealot with leadership ability, vision, and motivational qualities are bound to succeed. Excellent support from top executives and senior managers also ensures the availability of resources, employee motivation, and rewards required to sustain continuous improvements.

Focus on Error-Prevention Philosophy

Making the transition to the new error-prevention philosophy requires managers and employees to alter their approach to solving problems, behave differently, change work habits, and participate with a positive attitude in new, more effective ways of providing quality products and services. Changing attitudes, behavior, and cultural values to encourage acceptance of a new total quality philosophy takes more than speeches from managers and consultants.

The key elements of successful attitude and behavioral change involve effective, focused leadership; communication; and reinforcement with rewards. The management team should present one voice when communicating goals, expectations, and initial change elements. Effective, open communication will reduce anxiety and fear of change. The communication must include progress toward quality goals and feedback from customers to complement the new quality- and customer-oriented culture.

Here are suggestions for enterprises embarking on transition actions. The enterprises should decide on the initial changes and the timing of these changes. Initial changes should focus on creating awareness of quality, overcoming resentment, and creating passion for excellence. Cultural change should be initiated by the chief executive office but should also involve lower level managers and employees. Each employee must understand what is expected. Each work output must satisfy the customer's requirements, needs, and wants. Involve every member of the business unit team in identifying areas for quality improvement. Team participation usually minimizes anxiety and resentment.

Accountability for results and actions also has to be part of the reward system. Accountability measures for quality, revenue, and cost should be tracked, analyzed, and effectively used for improvement.

Establish a network of effective communication at all levels. Communication can be through written or visual material. Special reports on quality, bulletins, and meetings should be set up to review issues. Department meetings, videotapes, posters, cartoons, and management memoranda are all vehicles for the dissemination of quality-related information. A special instruction or communication on quality from the chief executive officer should be disseminated throughout the enterprise. Managers and employees should be kept informed of the latest developments in quality through conferences, journals, continuous education and training, and research activities. Also, communicate the cost of quality, productivity loss, and feedback from customers to managers and nonmanagers. Provide heightened quality awareness with emphasis on understanding and developing customer/supplier relationships.

Provide ongoing motivation to encourage individuals to support the new error prevention quality philosophy. Leadership becomes a key factor in motivating individuals to higher levels of achievement and turning them into avid supporters of the total quality improvement efforts.

Competitiveness Through Total Quality Solution

One of the required elements of a customer- and market-driven enterprise is to focus on competing through total quality solution. The total quality solution should address design aspects of product and services, product quality, service quality, and quality of management. Quality has value to suppliers and vendors, producers, consumers, process owners, and internal and external customers. Suppliers and vendors view quality as a measure of how well the products and services meet requirements and specifications. Producers view quality in terms of "fitness for use": the ability to process and produce with less rework, less scrap, minimal downtime, and high productivity. From the consumers' viewpoints, quality means reliability, durability, and availability of products and services without continuous repairs, rework, and failures. A customer- and market-driven enterprise should view quality in the following ways:

- Quality is error-free performance of people and mechanisms.
- Quality is preventing errors and defects of all kinds.
- Quality is safe performance and protection against all unsafe conditions.
- Quality is prompt action through delivery and time scheduling.
- Quality is efficient and effective performance.
- Quality is purchased products and services that are defect free.
- Quality is correct problem diagnosis through sound data analysis.
- Quality is getting rid of problems through correct remedies.
- Quality is obtaining reliable products and services.
- Quality is courteous, reliable, and trustworthy behavior.

Market-driven quality could play a key role in total customer satisfaction and affects the attitudes and buying patterns of customers. Excellent quality products and services could create satisfied customers who will continue to use the products or services and recommend them to others. Such satisfied customers bring additional revenue to the enterprise. Poor quality usually creates dissatisfied customers. The poor product or service creates a bad reputation that quickly spreads in the marketplace. Customers stop buying such a product or service, and new customers are lost. Usually, a competitive product or service with better quality takes advantage of dissatisfied and lost customers. This has a

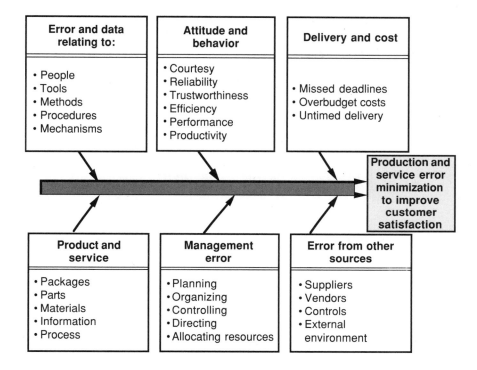

Figure 1.5: Typical Errors to Be Controlled in a Production and Service Work Environment

negative impact on growth, profitability, and increase in market share. Figure 1.5 shows the types of errors that should be corrected at the source of production or service for total customer satisfaction. The focus should be on error prevention and defect elimination. The goal is to have zero defects at the customer door.

Focus on Design and Product Quality

Quality obtained through changes in design parameters should also be addressed by a customer- and market-driven enterprise. Differences in quality can result from differences in size, materials and equipment used, reliability, and temperature. Quality of conformance measures how well the product conforms to specifications and tolerances required by the design. Such factors as training, the production process, motivation levels, procedures, and quality assurance systems can affect the quality of conformance. Quality characteristics typify the variety of uses of a given product. The quality characteristics may be of several types: behavioral or ethical (fairness, honesty, and courtesy), sensory (color, taste, appearance), time oriented (serviceable, reliable, and maintainable), and commercial (warranty).

Improvements in quality are therefore made by examining the design and conformance phases with their associated characteristics through the application of appropriate techniques and methods, including changes in design, timing, inspection procedures, and process control procedures. Quality, when viewed as conformance to specifications, has great potential as an effective improvement strategy; however, this can result in a lack of commitment to quality by members of an organization who do not acknowledge the present situation.

Focus on Quality of Services

Another aspect of quality for a customer- and market-driven enterprise to focus on is quality of services: the total satisfaction of requirements of internal and external customers receiving a service in a timely fashion at minimum cost. The measure also pertains to both tangible and intangible elements of service offered by individuals, operational units, and the total enterprise. Quality of service also involves physical factors, such as quality of products used for services, as well as the behavior and attitudes of persons rendering services to the customer. Unlike product quality, which focuses on the level of relevance, uniformity, and dependability, service quality is a function of the production, delivery, and consumption processes. Most services have more tangible elements. It is very difficult to apply quantitative standards and measures to services. The quantitative standards that are usually available are applied in an indirect manner. Unspoken standards also exist in service quality management. The standards usually include human attributes such as humility, empathy, courtesy, respect, care, and patience. The quantitative and nonquantitative standards in service quality were summarized in Table 1.1. Usually, services are tacked onto quality of products, so they receive little attention. The winning organizations are those that pay attention to all types of quality. One major drawback in the service industry is that there are very few professionals working to improve service quality. Product quality tends to dominate service quality, especially in small and medium enterprises.

Improving the quality of services requires attention to physical factors such as quality of products used for services and addressing the behavior and attitudes of the employees rendering services directly to the customer. It also involves providing a mechanism for end user feedback and improvement.

Focus on Quality of Management and Supervision

To improve management practices and procedures, a customer- and market-driven enterprise must focus on improving the quality of management and supervision. This pertains to how well managers and supervisors of operational work units are able to plan, organize, control, delegate, and direct employees to products and services of the highest quality and then deliver them at the right time at a competitive price. It also pertains to how well managers are able to motivate people to do their best, provide a good working environment and tools, and reward accomplishments. Excellent quality of management and supervision can be achieved though attention to details and actions that address both people- and product-oriented issues.

Focus on Personal Quality

Every employee in a customer- and market-driven enterprise should be encouraged to focus on improving personal quality. Personal quality pertains to the passion for quality excellence and total customer satisfaction. It involves continuously demonstrating the right attitude toward the customer, the job, the supplier, and work teams and support for the enterprise's quality goals and objectives. Personal quality also relates to how well an individual's knowledge, skill, and experience are used to produce excellent goods and services. As shown in Figure 1.6, improving personal quality requires emphasis on personal traits as well as technical and other capabilities. The organization's climate and quality of management can also affect personal quality. Participative management is conducive to improvement in personal quality.

Focus on Productivity, Efficiency, and Effectiveness

A customer- and market-driven enterprise should pay attention to productivity, which is a measure of how well resources are used to produce output. It relates output to input and integrates performance aspects of

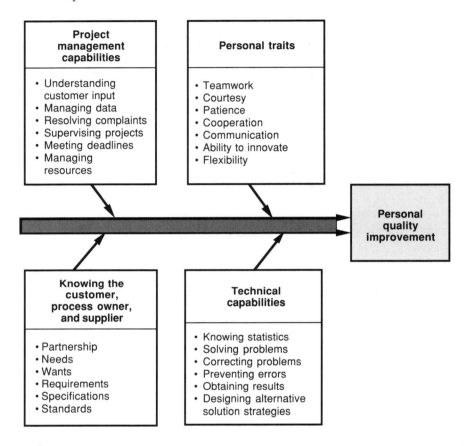

Figure 1.6: Elements Involved in Improving Personal Quality

quality, efficiency, and effectiveness. Productivity does not necessarily imply that people should work harder but that they should work smarter with new or better tools, techniques, processes, resources, and ideas. Productivity technologies are essential for making the most of production and service processes. Management of productivity can provide the basis for higher real earnings for employees. The reduction of goods and services might allow increases in wages without any offsetting gains in overall productivity. Higher productivity enables consumers to pay lower prices for goods and services because the cost of production is reduced by eliminating rework and making gains in productivity. The continuous management of productivity facilitates more effective utilization of resources. More goods and services should be produced for reasonable amounts of expended resources. The public may also realize greater social benefits through increased public revenues derived from the productivity gains.

Productivity management integrates performance aspects of quality to reduce rework and scrap, provide better utilization of tools and equipment, and require less work-in-process inventory, which should in turn lead to even higher productivity. Productivity technologies and the level of productivity growth can make a difference in a competitive world economy. The output/input ratio obtained from two similar tasks, processes, and firms can vary significantly, depending on how well productivity technologies are applied.

A customer- and market-driven enterprise should use breakthroughs in technology, research, and development to improve productivity. The enterprise's research should be applied to discoveries of potential value to the firm in developing new products or cost-reducing technology. Part of the research and development (R&D) effort should be focused on engineering and logistics needed to translate useful inventions into commercially feasible production processes or new products.

Emphasis should also be placed on educating workers (both professional and nonprofessional). This has a reciprocal relationship, in that technologically progressive enterprises offer greater opportunities in more skilled and professional occupations. Also, workers with higher levels of education and training tend to make larger contributions to advancing technology. The enterprise should also focus on the following areas to achieve improvement in productivity: quality of management, new technologies, organizational structure, privilege given to workers for innovation and cost reduction, and quality of retraining programs.

The definition of productivity should not be confused with efficiency and effectiveness. Effectiveness is a measure of the output of an operational unit. It is a measure of how well an operational unit is able to accomplish its objective. Efficiency is a measure of the degree to which an operational unit utilizes appropriate resources in the right manner. The four types of productivity measures recommended at the enterprise level are

- *Comprehensive productivity:* the ratio of tangible and intangible output to all tangible and intangible input factors

- *Total productivity:* the ratio of total measurable output to all measurable input factors

- *Total factor productivity:* the ratio of total measurable output to the sum of associated labor and capital (factor) inputs
- *Partial productivity:* the ratio of total measurable output to one class of input

Productivity measurement technologies are means of identifying the performance of people, processes, products, and services. The measures are used to focus on specific areas for improvement, process evaluation, and planning projections.

Customer- and Market-Driven Quality and Productivity Technologies

A customer- and market-driven enterprise should use quality and productivity technologies, tools, techniques, methods, and measurements to plan, develop, design, control, evaluate, and improve products and services. Quality technologies are means of protecting the customer through delivery of defect-free products and services. This is done by using the quality technologies to identify critical processes that control the performance of the final products or services. Quality and productivity technologies are required for the optimization of input, process, and output. These technologies also help manage and optimize the requirements of a production or service system as specified in Figure 1.7. The technologies are continuously applied to the inputs, transformation process, and outputs to satisfy market requirements and organizational needs.

Summary

There are several basic requirements for achieving a genuine customer- and market-driven enterprise. The focus on enhancing value, excellence, and total customer satisfaction should be maintained throughout the enterprise. Attention should be paid to management with facts and customer data, quality first, proper planning, and effective utilization of human resources. Management must support programs that satisfy customers and provide adequate compensation and rewards to employees and shareholders.

The task is to have everyone take responsibility for quality and customer satisfaction. The integration of a customer-oriented approach to every business issue and creation of a total quality culture are important

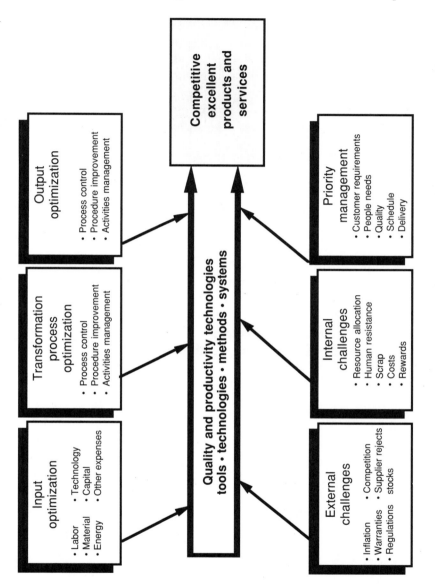

Figure 1.7: Elements Involved in Production and Service System Optimization

elements for success. Everyone should also take responsibility for understanding and satisfying the requirements of internal and external customers. The commitment to productivity and quality excellence means that a total quality culture exists in which everyone constantly considers the quality of their work and how it is reflected in the final output. This also requires that workers be allowed to have control, responsibility, and decision latitude for a variety of activities such as maintenance, information control, quality, process analysis, service, production, and resource allocation.

The total quality culture that is recommended involves continuous improvement focus and obsession with quality excellence and customer satisfaction. The customer- and market-driven enterprise team should focus on implementing new ideas that lead to improvement. The structure of the enterprise should encourage creativity and innovation to continuously improve the ways in which customers' needs are fulfilled. Resources should be provided by top management to improve products and services provided to the customer. The philosophy of continuous improvement should be communicated as a way of life for everyone in the enterprise. This requires that every member of the organization have a clear understanding of the importance of competing through excellent quality products and services.

Total Quality Management and Continuous Improvement of Work Processes

The quest for quality excellence and total customer satisfaction involves a race with no finish line. Both management and employees should focus on continuous improvement of all work processes to improve quality, productivity, and overall effectiveness.

Total quality management (TQM) is an evolving competitive strategy for continuous improvement of products, processes, and services to enhance quality, reduce cost, and improve productivity and total customer satisfaction. TQM involves the quantitative, nonquantitative, behavioral, management statistics, economics, and systems engineering tools and methods to control all production and service processes of an enterprise to satisfy customer needs and requirements. It is based on the principle that continuous quality improvement creates increased productivity, lower cost, stronger competitive position, and increases in market share and profitability. As shown in Figure 2.1, TQM involves several elements, including management participation and development, employee involvement and the use of action teams, supplier certification and training, education and training of the work force, emphasis on total customer satisfaction, partnership between suppliers, process owners, and customers, use of appropriate recognition and reward systems and an ongoing focus on use of problem-solving tools to improve performance, quality, and productivity.

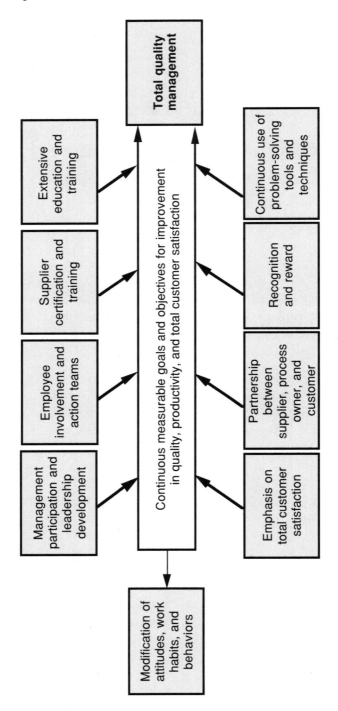

Figure 2.1: TQM Elements

TQM demands commitment and discipline. It relies on people, involves everyone, and requires a participative management approach. It achieves continuous improvement through focus on the processes that create products and services. The products and services are key indicators of the effectiveness of their processes. Continuous process improvement is the TQM hallmark. Commitment from top management and the work force is required for successful implementation. Such commitment should include: providing resources to support improvement projects, ongoing focus on cost reduction and customer satisfaction, and ongoing education and training of the work force. TQM practices are based on consistent improvement goals and objectives geared for every aspect of the enterprise. TQM also focuses on improving suppliers' capabilities through education and technical assistance, and more creative ways of improving suppliers' processes. Another requirement for success is communication. Unfettered cross-functional vertical and horizontal communication is recommended. TQM practices aim to remove communication barriers and process bottlenecks between management and the work force and between operational work units. To grasp the concepts of TQM, the essential tools, techniques, and skills must be institutionalized at all levels of the enterprise. Workers and managers must be taught planning and goal-setting techniques to analyze customer and supplier needs, expectations, and feedback. TQM employs the best available management practices, technologies, tools, and techniques to satisfy the needs of the customer. It creates teamwork and constructive working relationships that recognize people as the enterprise's greatest asset and their talents as the key element of success. It involves every individual in improving all work processes and builds and sustains a culture committed to continuous process improvement.

Continuous improvement is a TQM hallmark. Continuous improvement is the act of enhancing value and excellence constantly and forever. The philosophy of continuous improvement leads enterprises, teams, and individuals to constantly improve outdated processes, procedures, technologies, systems, and work habits to reduce waste and focus on error prevention and defect elimination. The continuous improvement process consists of groups of activities that complement each other and provide the support structure and environment for improving performance and achieving the highest levels of quality and competitiveness. Improvements may be made in these areas: quality of incoming materials, responsiveness to internal and external customers, cycle time reduction, reducing errors and defects at the source of production or service, enhancing value to the customer through improved product and service attributes, and improving efficient and effective use of all resources. Adopting the philosophy of continuous improvement means one is not satisfied with the status quo or content with getting by with old methods.

Continuous improvement demands regular cycles of planning, measurement, evaluation, and improvement. The improvement process must have quantitative and qualitative approaches for assessing progress and for implementing future improvements. It also should have key elements to help work teams and individuals accept change and make continuous improvement a necessary way of life. Continuous improvement should not be referred to as a new buzzword or fad. It is a way of thinking, planning, working, and striving for excellence in everything that is done. The continuous improvement journey involves a race with no finish line. It is a journey that is both demanding and satisfying; demanding because it is ongoing, and satisfying because as the journey continues, innovative ways are employed to enhance skills, processes, procedures, and technologies that help improve work processes. It also requires a long-term commitment from the entire staff of the enterprise, for it takes time to change the personality of an enterprise from reaction to prevention.

Why Focus on Total Quality Management and Continuous Improvement of Work Processes?

Enterprises worldwide are experiencing a customer-driven competition. The availability of high-quality, low-cost products and services competing for a share of the market has stimulated a search for a new business strategy. The continuous improvement philosophy is the right strategy for achieving excellence in product and service quality, productivity and performance, organizational effectiveness, and total customer satisfaction. Short-term financial success or profitability is no longer good enough for an enterprise operating in a competitive world economy. Achieving long-term success through continuous improvement of the work process is the right strategy. Continuous improvement is driven not only by the objective of long-term profitability and growth but also by the need to be responsive to competitive pressures in the marketplace. The response should focus on superior quality and competitive price. An enterprise can achieve the following benefits through TQM and continuous improvement.

A focus on TQM and continuous improvement enables an enterprise to understand and satisfy ever-changing customer requirements through better processes that provide excellent goods and services. It also enables an enterprise to stay ahead of the competition through continual promotion of innovative ideas for better products, services, and technologies. The improvement process also helps an enterprise continually benchmark products and services against those of the competition. Regular cycles of improvement strategies are then developed and implemented to stay ahead of the competition.

Continuous improvement of work processes has been proven to improve market share, reduce cost, improve effectiveness, and enhance total customer satisfaction. Surviving, competing, and winning in a competitive world economy requires focus on a never-ending improvement process. The enterprise, team, or individual that believes the quality challenge that lies ahead is greater than any it has faced to date will adopt the philosophy of continuous improvement.

Every function and every individual—suppliers, customers, managers, supervisors, employees, and unions—should focus on TQM and continuous improvement of all work processes to improve quality, productivity, and overall enterprise effectiveness. Teamwork between individuals and functional areas of the enterprise must be encouraged. Partnership between suppliers, process owners, and customers is required to embark on a successful TQM and continuous improvement journey.

How to Implement the Total Quality Management Concept and Continuous Improvement Philosophy

The keys to effective implementation of the TQM and continuous improvement philosophy are presented in Figure 2.2. A discussion of each essential element of implementation follows.

Top Management Commitment and Participation

Top management's sincere commitment, support, and leadership in continuous improvement efforts are key requirements for success. This active support and commitment should focus on the eight success factors summarized in Figure 2.3. Top managers should recognize the business environment they are in to provide clear goals and objectives for guiding

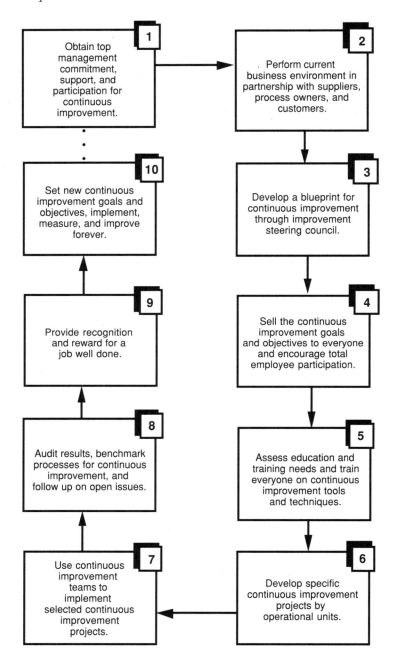

*Figure 2.2: Ten Essential Elements for Implementing TQM
and the Continuous Improvement Philosophy*

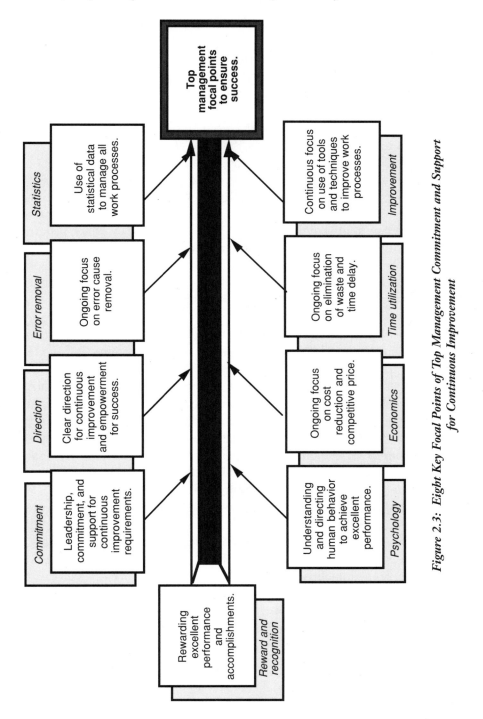

Figure 2.3: Eight Key Focal Points of Top Management Commitment and Support for Continuous Improvement

the enterprise team's continuous improvement efforts. Top managers must make a physical, mental, and philosophical commitment to quality and total customer satisfaction if there is to be a comprehensive quality and customer satisfaction initiative. This type of commitment is generally prompted by an awareness and acceptance of the need for change. If there is no strong commitment from top management, priorities will shift before results can be achieved.

Evidence of commitment is shown through ongoing support of quality and customer satisfaction improvement projects. Top managers must monitor, encourage, and reward those who actively improve products and processes. Commitment also involves allocating resources to correcting common causes in the system that are responsible for poor quality. When long-standing systemic issues are identified which require resources to be redirected for resolution, management must respond. It is also important that specific goals and objectives be set to direct employee efforts. Employees must understand how their efforts support the company's strategic plan and must be held accountable for making a contribution.

Top managers must also be committed to utilizing statistics, measurement techniques, and data collection to control variability in human, mechanized, and automated performance. This represents a philosophical commitment that is key to success. The top management team must continue to grow, develop, and change as the culture changes. The growth involves studying, understanding, and positively directing human behavior toward excellent performance. The responsibility for managing the economics surrounding the business remains with top management. Costs and prices must be kept at levels that allow affordable products and services to be delivered while the company remains profitable.

Two key elements that must be continually reinforced and demonstrated by top managers are a commitment to minimizing delay time, idle time, wasted time, and lost time and to utilizing the methods, procedures, and processes required to ensure that the products and services rendered are of exceptional quality.

Finally, top managers must be committed to authorizing employees to take corrective action for preventing errors, defects, and delays at every level of the organization. The following steps should be taken to ensure the involvement of top managers in TQM and continuous improvement efforts.

Step one: Train top managers on continuous improvement tools and techniques, managing change, and creating a total quality culture. Involve top managers in continuous improvement training for middle managers, supervisors, and other professionals.

Step two: Make continuous quality, productivity, and total customer satisfaction improvement the chief executive officer's personal mission. Encourage top executive participation in the enterprise's continuous improvement steering committee to oversee continuous improvement project plans, allocate resources, and monitor progress.

Step three: Require annual continuous improvement plans from line executives and managers. Such plans should depict a blueprint for comprehensive implementation of specific improvement projects. The plan should include specifics on training requirements, customer satisfaction improvement, supplier management, information analysis, process control and data management, employee job satisfaction and human resource issues, benchmarking of competitors, and cost-of-quality estimate for each business unit.

Step four: Include discussions about TQM and continuous improvement projects in all staff meetings. Top managers should participate in continuous improvement projects, recognition events for quality excellence, and the enterprise's suggestion program for continuous improvement.

Step five: Put executives and top managers in touch with customers, suppliers, and professional organizations. An executive will have a greater appreciation of the requirements, needs, and problems of customers and suppliers if one-on-one contact is made. Such contact also provides a unique opportunity for the executive to exchange ideas on continuous improvement goals, objectives, and specific projects. Outside contact with professional organizations also provides positive exposure for the enterprise and professional validation of new ideas.

The TQM and continuous improvement philosophy must be an integral part of top management's vision, practice, and personal mission. Organizations with a top management zealot who possesses leadership ability, vision, and motivational qualities are bound to succeed. Excellent support from top executives and senior managers also ensures the availability of resources, employee motivation, and rewards required to sustain continuous improvements at all levels of the enterprise.

Current Business Environment Assessment

The current business environment is assessed to determine areas of strength and weakness so that a strategy for continuous improvement implementation can be developed. The assessment of the operational environment serves as an educational step for the top management team and the improvement teams by defining the current state. The assessment provides a baseline on product, process, and information quality and human resource utilization. One of the important elements of success is understanding supplier and customer requirements. The supplier plays a key role in determining the quality of inputs. The customer is the final judge of the quality and competitiveness of goods and services. The goal is to find methods of identifying supplier requirements and identifying customer needs, wants, and desires and translating them into product and service requirements. Those who create the output and those who receive it should agree on clear, measurable goals for the work. To capture the requirements of suppliers and customers in products and services, producers must begin to listen extensively to the voice of the customer.

This begins with obtaining marketing information and customer perception data on existing and competing products and services. This data collection provides the baseline required to develop a clear understanding of customer demands, and data must be collected on an ongoing basis. The next step is to break down the product and service system into part or process characteristics and determine qualitative and quantitative issues and target values for the defined characteristics. These values must then be compared to the customer baseline data. To compare customer data to product data, customer requirements and characteristics must be specified in like terms. Customer requirements and market information must be analyzed and the data synthesized for relevance. Interrelationships between characteristics should be considered at this time. Once this critical analysis is complete, the final step is to fully define product and service characteristics and technical measurements that meet customer requirements.

The assessment of the business environment must be continuous. This requires ongoing partnership with suppliers and customers which provides the basis for total understanding of market requirements, needs, and wants. The following are suggestions for enhancing partnership between suppliers, process owners, and customers.

First, maintain ongoing communication with customers and suppliers. This requires one-on-one contact, an on-line communication channel, telephone contact, and periodic site visits.

Perform periodic surveys to assess the degree of customer satisfaction. Use survey feedback to pinpoint areas for improvement. Provide feedback to customers on improvements achieved in product and service offerings.

Also, encourage customer participation in developing quality excellence strategies for new products and services. Encourage suppliers to participate in implementing a quality excellence and total customer satisfaction program. This can be useful when suppliers' commodities are essential to the products and services delivered.

The assessment of the current business environment must be comprehensive and should provide a baseline on product, process, and information quality and human resource utilization. Major areas to focus on are as follows:

- *Leadership and culture:* senior management's success in creating quality values and building the values into the company's operational philosophy.

- *Quality of information utilization and analysis:* effectiveness of the company's collection and analysis of quality improvement and planning.

- *Strategic quality planning:* effectiveness of the company's integration of the customer's quality requirements into its business plan.

- *Human resource utilization:* success of the company's efforts to realize the full potential of the work force for quality management.

- *Quality assurance results:* effectiveness of the company's systems for assuring quality control of all its operations and in integrating control with continuous quality improvement. Demonstration of quality excellence is based on quantitative measures and results.

- *Customer satisfaction:* effectiveness of a company's utilization and integration of new technology into new and mature products and processes.

- *Innovation process management:* ability and commitment of a company to encourage and manage innovation at all levels.

- *Supplier management:* the company's success in encouraging and developing a supplier network that utilizes effective quality assurance and management techniques and controls.

A review of these areas provides the basis for understanding the enterprise's quality culture, technical systems, management philosophy, products and services, and ability and commitment to meet customer requirements. The organizational assessment should encompass analysis of surveys, interviews, and data collection efforts. It should conclude with prioritized recommendations to target the improvement strategy.

Blueprint for TQM and Continuous Improvement

The enterprise's improvement strategy should be developed with knowledge gained from the current business environment assessment just discussed. A steering council consisting of senior managers and/or their representatives should develop a blueprint for TQM and continuous improvement. This TQM and continuous improvement steering council is a process improvement designer and catalyst which prepares the enterprise for change and provides specific goals and objectives for improvement. The council also helps direct the implementation of continuous improvement projects.

Developing an effective strategy to direct the implementation will require vision and breakthrough thinking on the part of top management. Breakthrough thinking will occur through an effective orientation and education plan for top management on the concepts of TQM and continuous improvement. The team should then develop a mission statement and strategic goals with input from employees, customers, and suppliers. These goals will be used along with the results of the stage-one assessment to develop a phased improvement strategy. The team must share this strategy with all employees. This stage may take six months to two years. During that time, it is important to keep employees aware of activities and help them stay motivated toward change. This stage is probably the most important of all. Developing a clear focus and the collaborative involvement of the top management team are the keys to success.

The blueprint must encompass a long-range strategy for continuous improvement in quality productivity and total customer satisfaction that covers a minimum of four product cycles or 12 years, whichever is longer. The enterprise management team and nonmanagers must understand the blueprint to the point that they can develop, at various operational levels, short-range plans (one to four years) to ensure that their operational activities support the long-range strategy.

These short-range continuous improvement plans should be included in the annual business plan, and each operational unit should be measured throughout the year on how well it is meeting these commitments. The measures used at the operational unit levels should include, but not be limited to, the following: quality, productivity, customer satisfaction indices, costs, delivery times and schedules, savings per employee, resource improvement ratios, and growth in market share. The enterprise's continuous improvement goals and objectives should be concise, clear, and presented in a manner that everyone can understand. Some companies have been able to summarize their goals and objectives on index cards in wording that is easy for all employees to understand and remember.

Continuous Improvement Goals and Objectives

It takes time to involve everyone in the continuous improvement effort. Total quality and productivity improvement cannot be achieved overnight. Implementation of continuous improvement goals and objectives requires total participation and involvement of the work force. The ability of managers and supervisors to sell the blueprint and the need for continuous improvement is critical. When the management team is involved through hands-on day-to-day participation, employee involvement is easy to obtain. When employees see upper and middle management involvement, participation in, and dedication to continuous improvement efforts, they will support and participate in them as well.

The selling of the TQM and continuous improvement goals and objectives to everyone should also focus on why they are needed, the resources to support improvement projects, assurance of fair reward and recognition for everyone, and the overall benefits for the enterprise. To achieve total participation, barriers to communication must be removed both laterally and vertically. Total involvement of everyone through opportunities to participate in continuous improvement projects is essential to eliminating communications barriers. The TQM and continuous improvement project's focus at the first line and department level should also be to provide a forum for sharing knowledge among team members.

Another method of encouraging employee participation is the continuous improvement suggestion program. This provides a means for each individual to contribute ideas to the success of the overall goals and objectives. Such a suggestion program must also have in place measures for success and mechanisms for recognizing individual contributions to improvement.

Education and Training Needs

Figure 2.4 shows recommended training profiles for enterprises. The assessment of education and training needs should be comprehensive in approach and is a key element of the overall improvement strategy. The assessment should include reviewing the requirements for new hires, formal and on-the-job training approaches, and career enhancement opportunities. Interviews should be conducted with employees, including managers, to determine the effectiveness of current training programs and to define training needs associated with TQM, process understanding, technical tools, leadership development, and participative management. Current training programs should be audited for content and relevance. The recommendations that follow the assessment must include in-house and external training opportunities focused on the continual development of employees at all levels.

Once education and training needs have been identified, all employees should be trained on the required continuous improvement tools and techniques. While training requirements may vary at the operational and individual levels, it is essential for everyone to make short-term

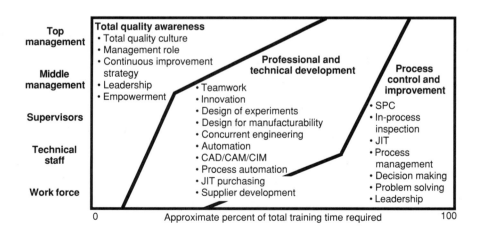

Figure 2.4: Recommended Continuous Improvement
Training Profile for Enterprises

and long-term contributions to the continuous improvement efforts. Training sets the stage for the awareness required for cultural change. It also provides required skills and knowledge to address specific problems. The training effort should be extended to suppliers and customers within the framework of business relationships. The key objective of the enterprise's education and training program is to enable employees to contribute effectively to the continuous improvement process. The following approaches are recommended for deploying education and training needs.

- *Strategic:* The annual business plan which encompasses the annual quality plan for all levels of the enterprise should be used to develop specific types of training for employees to support the continuous improvement initiatives.

- *Universal:* The continuous improvement steering committee determines specific ongoing training required for all employees so they will be active participants in the continuous improvement process.

- *Customized:* The management team examines unique or specific needs and then provides customized training utilizing internal or external resources based on the individual situation.

- *Individual:* Through programs for encouraging active employee participation, all employees review their development needs and, in concert with their managers, define and implement individual education and training.

- *Focus training processes and aids:* Most enterprises train the trainers to reduce the costs of training. Some use supervisors to do the training. The training process should emphasize a diversified program of courses for all employees. Suggested areas are specified in Figure 2.4. Tuition aid for college course work is also recommended for encouraging continuous management and employee development.

TQM and Continuous Improvement Projects

Specific TQM and continuous improvement projects are developed for operational units with the knowledge gained from assessment of the current business environment. Through the suggestion program, individuals or operational units can also bring forward specific projects on which to focus. Collaboration and cooperation among functional areas is the key to the success of this step. Improvement projects identified by operational units and individuals should be prioritized according to their potential for cost reduction, defect elimination, and overall enterprise effectiveness. The availability of resources should also be considered when selecting improvement projects. All improvement ideas should be reviewed carefully, because failure to implement a sample could lead to substantial losses of savings in resources, time, and quality improvement. Those who contributed the improvement ideas should help in the prioritization and final selection.

Continuous Improvement Teams

As shown in Figure 2.5, the TQM and continuous improvement team consists of individuals representing each operational unit involved in the process. The team works across functional boundaries. The group meets regularly to identify, analyze, and resolve specific problems of improving quality, productivity, and total customer satisfaction. A successful continuous improvement team must (1) use a participative approach to goals, objectives and vision setting, (2) allow open sharing of ideas, (3) encourage open communication among team members, and (4) provide team reward and recognition. The roles and responsibilities of the improvement facilitator, team leader, and team members are described in Figure 2.5.

It is important to note that the implementation of continuous improvement projects occurs over time. It involves continuously assessing progress, accepting the evolution of innovative approaches, and restructuring and correcting to ensure progress toward objectives. A continuous improvement steering council should be formed to monitor and guide project implementation. This council can determine requirements for tailored orientation and education for all employees, assist with the development of organized employee action teams, and recommend reorganization when appropriate. Its ongoing responsibility is to assist with assessment, update, and revision of the continuous improvement strategy as required. The following guidelines are provided to help continuous improvement teams.

Goal Setting

Members of the continuous improvement team should clearly define their goals and objectives. The mission of each team should be defined

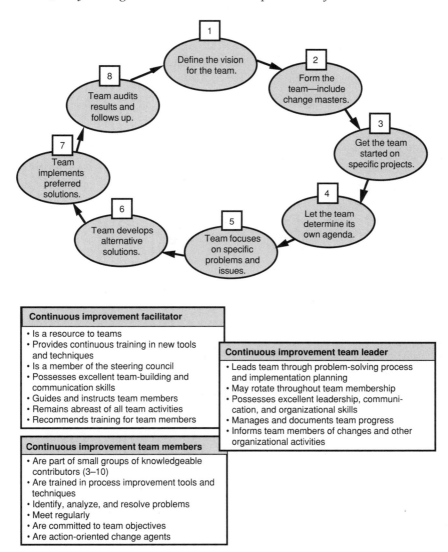

Figure 2.5: Steps to Form and Operate a Continuous Improvement Team and the Roles and Responsibilities of Team Members

without ambiguity. Each team member should be encouraged to create and focus on the vision of the improved process and operational unit. The goal is that no level of defect is acceptable. The team's improvement focus should be on every task, process, procedure, and policy for each operational unit. In setting the goals for improvement, the team should use a participative approach. The team should allow for productivity and quality goals that are measurable, attainable, and open to opportunity. Improvement goals should be prioritized, with measures in place for monitoring progress. A team consensus on the goals should be obtained and the goals then implemented.

Problem Analysis and Resolution

The goal of the continuous improvement team is to resolve new problems and initiate and implement improvement strategies that focus on error prevention and defect elimination. Problem analysis and resolution should happen at the source. The focus should be correcting process flaws through analysis of task parameters, inputs, processes, and outputs. Encourage the use of simple and effective tools for problem solving. The right tools and techniques are usually acquired through continuous education and training, cross training, and on-the-job training. Team members should train each other on new methods and techniques and cross train for multiple skills. Management support in providing the required information tools and techniques to do the job right is crucial. Such support should include all financial and technical resources required for successful completion of the project. One of the keys to successful problem analysis and resolution is the establishment of a work plan for each improvement project. The plan should cover schedule, cost, savings, resource requirements, and short-term and long-term focus. Establish a focus point for coordinating all improvement activities.

Teamwork and Communication Channels

Ongoing enhancement of communication channels should be available to team members at all levels. Encourage teamwork within operational work units and across functional boundaries. To avoid confusion, each team member's roles and responsibilities should be clearly defined at the operational and task levels. Provide support systems that facilitate decision making and problem solving at the source. Figure 2.6 presents a four-step process for successful continuous improvement team meetings. Team members must communicate effectively and regularly. Whenever they hold a meeting, its purpose should be defined and the specific agenda and time duration provided. The meeting should start on time and the minutes should be recorded. The closure should summarize key accomplishments, follow-up items, and acknowledgment of team members' contributions to the success of the meeting.

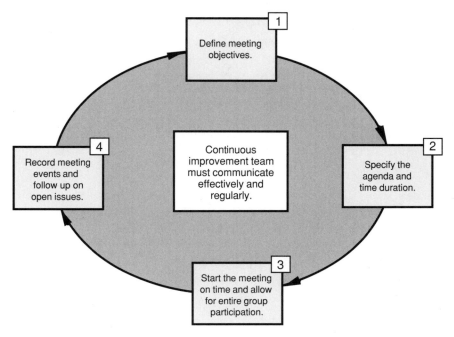

***Figure 2.6: Four-Step Approach to Successful Continuous
Improvement Team Meetings***

Team Recognition and Reward

Team members can recognize themselves by acknowledging the contributions of others to the success of improvement projects. In addition, management plays a critical role in this area. Managers and supervisors should provide feedback mechanisms for information among people, processes, and procedures, provide real-time recognition for a job well done, and share the gains from productivity and quality improvement among participating team members. Also, people can be motivated through additional responsibilities, a simple "thank-you" for a job well done, and meaningful job content, autonomy, and training to perform their duties. Rewards should be provided in a timely manner.

The implementation stage will require patience, risk taking, and investment in training, process improvement, technology, and professional third-party assistance. This methodology results in a continuously improving organization with processes in place to manage quality and productivity as required. The resulting payback is high-quality products and services and satisfied customers, which translate to bottom-line profits.

Auditing Results and Benchmarking Processes for Continuous Improvement

Once specific improvement projects have been implemented, the next step is to audit results and follow up on open issues. The actual results obtained should be compared with the specific goal and anticipated performance. All discrepancies should be identified and feedback provided to the continuous improvement team members for follow-up. One of the major difficulties experienced by most individuals and enterprises is how to measure the success of continuous improvement efforts. Tables 2.1

Table 2.1: Example of a Short-Term and Long-Term Continuous Improvement Goals for a Medium-Sized Company

Category	Initial continuous improvement goals	Long-term CI goals (four years)
Management	• Set continuous improvement goals. • Define metrics. • Plans to train all employees. • Provide regular, continuous process improvement focus at all levels.	• Institutionalize continuous improvement. • Train leaders in quality improvement. • Determine process output, yield, and predictability. • Implement natural cross-functional approaches. • Maintain total partnership with customers and suppliers.
Quality and reliability	• Evaluate and monitor SPC programs. • Benchmark and set new targets in all areas of performance. • Review all processes, procedures, and specifications.	• Maintain processes under control using SPC. • Be sure variability in all processes is well understood. • Predict outputs and outcomes. • Characterize products and processes up front. • Achieve zero defects in outgoing quality.
Innovation and technology management	• Design for manufacturability program. • Have cross-functional teams characterize processes. • Redefine technology transfer methodology. • Map product strategy to continuous improvement goals.	• Promote leading-edge capabilities. • Maintain successful, timely, predictable technology transfers. • Establish predominant, first-time success with timely and competitive products.
Productivity and cost reduction	• Review all processes against productivity goals. • Implement cost principles in equipment and materials. • Determine cost of nonconformance program. • Set process simplification and improvement objectives.	• Eliminate nonconformance costs. • Encourage and accept prevention costs willingly. • Understand and implement total cost analysis. • Keep new processes and tools in statistical control. • Help suppliers achieve and provide components to specifications. • Have reward system in place for process simplification.
Delivery and service	• Set 100% on-time delivery as the minimum acceptable. • Analyze all cycle time components. • Reexamine lead times to fit customer. • Determine requirements and world-class industry standards.	• Be sure customer and supplier partnerships prevail. • Have real-time data and communication links in place to globally support all customers. • Ensure that the sole source, JIT environment prevails. • Achieve and modify, as needed, cycle time goals.

and 2.2 present an example of areas to examine for continuous improvement and total quality management benchmarking. The types of standards that should be condensed are presented in Table 2.3.

To ensure proper audit results, establish a mechanism for circulating information among people, processes, and procedures. Implement a management information system. This system should incorporate a database on productivity and quality trends, issues, and key accomplishments. Data should be available to analysts and continuous improvement team members working to improve all key processes. Results of implementing continuous improvement projects should be benchmarked against those of competitors.

Benchmarking entails the search for industry best practices that lead to superior performance. It involves comparing all activities being done, all results being obtained, and all forms of strategic planning, means, and processes for doing work against those of the competitors. Benchmarking enables an enterprise to identify strengths and weaknesses compared to industry best practices, learn more efficient techniques and tools, and

Table 2.2: Total Quality Benchmarking

Continuous improvement (CI) and TQM category	Top management commitment	Obsession with excellence	Organization is customer driven	Customer satisfaction	Education and training	Employee involvement and participative management	Use of incentives	Use of CI tools
5	Continuous improvement is a natural behavior even during routine tasks.	Constant, relative improvement in quality, cost, and productivity is needed.	Customer satisfaction is the primary goal.	More customers state their intention to maintain a long-term business relationship.	Training in TQM tools is common among all employees.	Employees are involved in self-directing work groups.	Gain sharing or cross-functional teams are used.	Statistics is a common language among all employees.
4	Focus is on improving the system.	Cross-functional improvement teams are used.	Customer feedback is used in decision making.	Striving to improve value to customers is a routine behavior.	Top management understands and applies TQM principles.	Managers define limits and ask their groups to make decisions.	There are more team than individual incentives and rewards.	Design and other departments use SPC and CI techniques.
3	Adequate money and time are allocated to continuous improvement and training.	A TQM support system is set up and in use.	Tools are used to include customer wants and needs in product design.	Positive customer feedback and complaints are used to improve products and/or services.	Training programs are ongoing.	Managers present problems and get suggestions from employees before making any decisions.	Quality-related employee selections and promotion criteria are used.	SPC and CI tools are used to reduce variation.
2	Long- and short-term goals are balanced.	An executive steering committee is set up.	Customer needs and wants are known.	The customer's rating of the company is known.	A training plan is developed.	Managers present their ideas and invite questions before making any decisions.	An effective employee suggestion program is used.	CI tools are used in all processes.
1	• The traditional approach to quality, productivity, and performance improvement is used. —Inspection is a primary tool; thus control of defects and not prevention of defects is emphasized. —Better quality equals higher costs. —There is significant scrap and rework. —Quality control is found only in manufacturing departments. • There is a lack of teamwork and participative management.							

Standing — desired direction ▲

Table 2.3: Quantitative and Nonquantitative Standards in Service

Nonquantitative Standards	Quantitative Standards
• Responsiveness	• Defect rates
• Empathy	• Mean time to provide service
• Respect	• Repair time
• Conformance to customer requirements	• Waiting time
• Conformance to organizational goals and procedures	• Transaction time
• Patience	• Turnover rates
• Courtesy	• Time required to perform task
• Humility	• Time spent replacing unacceptable purchase
• Acceptable manner	• Mean time before failure
• Looks	• Deviation from arrival times
	• Deviation from departure times
	• Delivery times
	• Replacement costs
	• Shipping

implement them to stay ahead of the competition. Good benchmarking analysis produces two types of information: (1) quantitative data used to measure performance and to set future targets, and (2) qualitative information on key success factors that explain how other enterprises became best-in-class in that function. Either outside consultants or an internal continuous improvement team can perform benchmarking. The following six-step approach, shown in Figure 2.7, is recommended.

Step one: Identify continuous improvement functions or categories (management, technology, quality, productivity, process steps, cost, delivery and schedule, strategic planning, customer satisfaction indices, supplier process, and information system). Also identify companies that are best in class in the selected areas for benchmarking. This may require

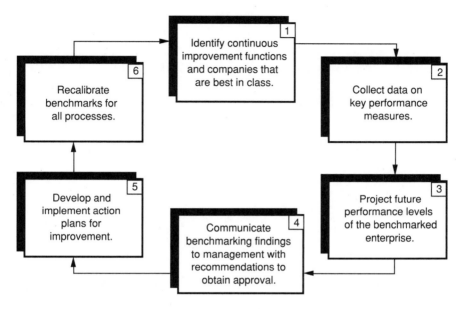

Figure 2.7: Six-Step Approach to Benchmarking

national and international competitive analysis, depending on the type, size, products, and services offered by the enterprise.

Step two: Identify and collect data on key performance measures. Review industry trends and select key measures that can be compared with other enterprises. Collect data on key measures. Describe management approaches that differ between enterprises, and identify key success factors.

Step three: Project future performance levels of the benchmarked enterprise over the short term (two years) and long term (five to ten years). Develop a plan to match or exceed the best-in-class performance level. Establish specific functional goals to reach the desired level of performance.

Step four: Communicate benchmarking findings, analysis, and recommendations to management for approval. Recommendations should identify specific areas of strengths and suggested improvements, as well as strategies to achieve excellence by functional area. After senior management review, communicate the recommendations to employees to build enthusiasm for the new continuous improvement goals.

Step five: Develop and implement action plans for improvement. For each specific objective defined, the continuous improvement team develops a step-by-step implementation plan. Collect data after a period of time to determine new performance levels. Make adjustments to the continuous improvement plans if the goals are not met. Implementation steps should also include a specific work plan with schedule dates, resources, expected benefits, and measures of performance.

Step six: Recalibrate benchmarks for all processes. Since the right focus for success is on continuous improvement of all work processes to improve value and excellence, the continuous improvement team should continue to reevaluate and update the benchmarks to ensure that they are based on the latest data. While this recalibration process for benchmarks might seen expensive, it is well worth the effort for any enterprise that aspires to be best in class in providing products and services.

Recognition and Reward for a Job Well Done

Management should make a sincere effort to provide real-time recognition for a job well done and share the gains from productivity and quality improvement. To keep the continuous improvement momentum alive, all participants who contribute to the success of specific projects must be rewarded. If this is not done, people become disenchanted. Money is not the only source of motivation; however, compensation and promotion should be related to excellent performance. Ideas implemented for continuous process improvement should be rewarded by management through awards, recognition among peers, bonus checks, additional technical challenge, and promotion. A simple "thank-you" for a job well done can go a long way toward reinforcing the commitment of an employee to the continuous improvement of quality, productivity, and performance. Encourage a suggestion program that rewards employees for their ideas. Whenever possible and appropriate, provide team reward and recognition. Team rewards also foster continued cooperation between functional areas and individuals.

TQM and Continuous Improvement Goals and Objectives

Continuous process improvement is a never-ending journey. New continuous improvement goals and objectives should be set and implemented. Ongoing focus on the efficient process that takes an input, adds value to it, and processes useful output is essential. The goals and objectives should involve any work or function performed in the enterprise. The new continuous improvement goals and objectives should also have a specific road map for implementation and key measures for evaluating short-term and long-term success.

Summary

The concepts of TQM and continuous improvement in processes, products, and services are central to all successful implementation of quality and productivity projects. The continuous improvement process consistently produces higher levels of performance through excellence in operations execution. As part of the continuous improvement effort, all material and information flow processes should be simplified. Also, all processes should be visible and predictable. This implies that variances should be minimized in the inputs and outputs of all operations. Everyone must be involved in the continuous improvement effort. Leaders and managers should demonstrate commitment to continuous improvement by example. Continuous improvement in productivity and quality requires attention to error prevention and ongoing problem resolution. Error prevention and problem solving require teamwork among all departments, groups, and employees. It is very important to ensure that those charged with productivity and quality improvement be trained to use continuous improvement techniques and tools.

Quality excellence through continuous improvement does not happen by accident. It requires the right work plans, effective tools and techniques, and commitment to providing excellent goods and services at competitive cost and quality. Excellent performance is always the result of good application of common sense, tools and techniques, high intention, sincere effort, intelligent directions, skillful execution, and teamwork. Quality excellence and customer satisfaction involve a race with no finish line. Success requires commitment from every member of the organization to contribute talents and skills to ongoing process improvement. Continuous improvement in quality, productivity, and customer satisfaction involves organized use of common sense and tools to find easier and better ways of doing work.

CHAPTER 3

Total Customer Satisfaction Management

A market-driven enterprise should focus on satisfying the customer, who is the ultimate judge of whether the price, delivery, and quality of goods and services are satisfactory.

Who Is the Customer?

The customer is the person or group that receives the work output. That work may be a product or a service. Within an enterprise, customers are recipients of process outputs performed by suppliers. Each customer then becomes the supplier in subsequent process steps. Ultimately, the output of this network is a product or service provided to an external customer.

The customer is the final arbiter of quality, value, and price of products and services. As shown in Figure 3.1, there are three types of customers: the self-unit customer, the internal customer, and the external customer. All individuals are self-unit customers of themselves. Self-inspection, a disciplined attitude, and a desire for excellence should be the way of life for everyone. Internal customers are those who receive output from one or more internal process owners. External customers receive the finished good or service from the firm as a whole. The inputs of all customers—self-unit, internal, and external—must be considered in the project management process. To achieve total customer satisfaction, the needs, wants, and priorities of customers must be incorporated in the design and development, manufacturing, and service stages. Emphasis on

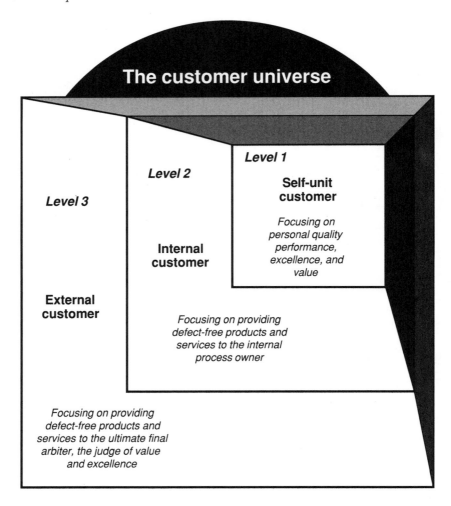

Figure 3.1: The Three Levels of Customer

excellent quality, performance, schedule and delivery, cost, and professional courtesy is a must for customer satisfaction.

Why Focus on Total Customer Satisfaction?

Attitudes and buying patterns of future customers can be affected by current customers' degree of satisfaction. Competitive quality creates satisfied customers who will continue to use the product or service and recommend it to others. Such satisfied customers bring additional revenue to the enterprise. Poor product and service quality causes bad publicity from dissatisfied customers which quickly spreads in the marketplace. The dissatisfied customer stops buying a product or service, and new customers are lost. This hurts the enterprise's growth, profitability, and market share.Usually, a competitive product or service with better quality takes advantage of these dissatisfied and lost customers.

Understanding the Market and Developing Customer-Driven Products and Services

The market analysis model (MAM) shown in Figure 3.2 depicts the elements involved in market analysis and segmentation. The key to success, however, is keeping in touch with the customer. Ongoing customer contact helps the enterprise stay informed about customers' perception of the marketplace, products, and services required. Products and services should be defined by each interaction with the customer and representatives of the enterprise. It may be extremely useful to encourage management

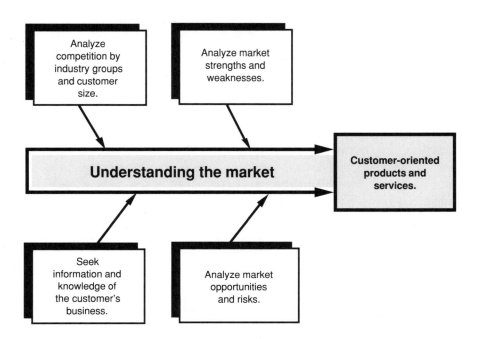

Figure 3.2: Elements of Market Analysis and Segmentation

representatives of customer companies to engage in ongoing communication of what is needed and when. The enterprise that analyzes its markets carefully, selects groups of customers whose needs match up best with its capabilities, and tailors its product offerings to do the best job of satisfying those needs will be rewarded with an increase in market share and better profit margins.

Understanding the customer involves knowing what is happening in the global marketplace by industry, subindustry, customer size, and consumer buying pattern. It involves knowing the customer's business, needs, desires, requirements, and resource base. It is also important to understand short-term opportunities and risks by market segments and the portions of the market segment that have dissatisfied customers. Markets must be prioritized and selected for long-term opportunities for growth.

Customer-Oriented Fast-Time-to-Market Model

A major challenge in the satisfaction of customers is deciding how to provide the right product in the right quantity at the right time, and at the right quality and price. The fast-time-to-market (FTTM) model presented in Figure 3.3 is offered to help enterprises achieve product and service objectives within increasingly shortened time spans without sacrificing quality and productivity. The four components of the model are described in the following sections.

Customer-Oriented Blueprint for Products and Services

The customer should be involved in developing a blueprint which describes the overall product and service FTTM objectives. At the firm and operational unit levels, short- and long-term objectives must be incorporated into overall business strategies. Such objectives must include how quality will be designed into new products and services, technology selection, specialization or embodiment, research and development investment and staffing, competitive timing, and quality and productivity improvement tools and techniques.

The first step in formulating the enterprise strategy involves customer participation in identifying all distinct technologies, subtechnologies, and quality improvement tools in the value chain. The potential relevant quality technologies in other industries are then identified. The second step involves determining which technologies are the most significant for competitive advantage and the likely path of change of key technologies.

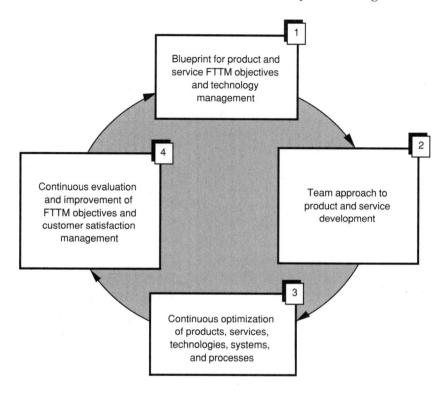

Figure 3.3: Fast-Time-to-Market Model

In the third step, the firm's relative capabilities in the important technologies and the cost of making improvements are assessed. The fourth and final step calls for selecting a strategy encompassing all important quality technologies that reinforce the firm's overall competitive strategy. The quality, productivity, and technology management and business unit strategy must complement and incorporate the objectives and goals specified in Figure 3.4. The means for achieving the objectives (reduced cycle time, cost reduction, quality improvement, flexibility, manufacturability, and reliability) must be specified. The means should address the management of product and service changes under conditions of rapid technological and social change, the interface between various organizations, the methods and tools for improving product and service quality, and adequate procedures, methodologies, and techniques for training the work force to the quality requirements of new products and services.

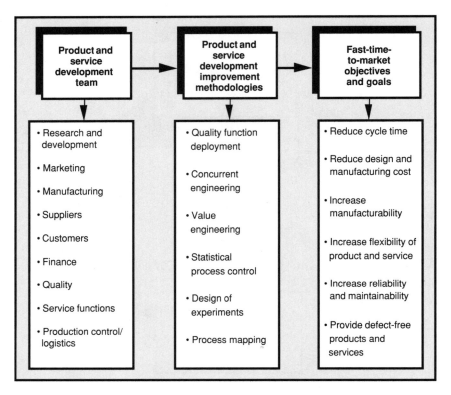

Figure 3.4: Focus Elements of Product and Service Development Team

Broadly managing the business basis requires looking beyond simple financial practices for business diversification and planning. Emphasis should be on a comprehensive strategy that encompasses short- and long-term objectives, all resources required for success, and FTTM goals. The blueprint for product and service objectives must be supported by top management. Formulation of objectives also requires the involvement of employees and every function of the organization. The blueprint must also reflect the strategic vision of the leaders and describe how the vision addresses product and service trend requirements.

Team Approach to Developing Quality Product and Service

Use interdisciplinary development teams to achieve product and service FTTM objectives. The team approach to product and service development enables suppliers, process owners, customers, designers, manufacturers, and marketing and service providers to communicate their needs and opinions on the product and service strategies under consideration. This concept allows all the functions involved to work together to fulfill the FTTM objectives. The benefits of teamwork in product and service development are well documented. Fortuna (1988) reported that engineering design changes have been reduced by 30–50 percent, product design cycles have been shortened by 30–50 percent, and start-up costs have been reduced 20–60 percent. These savings were attained despite the significant time by the product and service development team devoted to problem analysis and resolution. The team approach also improves cooperation, collaboration, and communication between work groups. The effective use of the right tools, techniques, and methodologies for product and service development is also recommended. Methodologies such as concurrent engineering, quality function deployment, statistical process control, design of experiments, and process mapping should be used to achieve excellent product and service development output.

Leadership of the product and service development teams is an important role. The team leader must be an experienced technical and people-oriented worker who focuses team effort on achieving the FTTM objectives through participative and proactive management styles.

PEAD Model

The Edosomwan PEAD model specified in Figure 3.5 is recommended. First, enterprise product development teams should pay attention to customer and supplier requirements and market information. Second, the teams should evaluate the effectiveness of the mechanisms in place to satisfy the customer and supplier requirements. Third, market information and data on customer and supplier requirements are synthesized for relevance. Fourth, product and service characteristics that meet customer and supplier requirements are developed. The PEAD model should be used to capture the requirements of the customer and supplier, and such requirements should be incorporated to produce excellent products and services.

Continuous Optimization of Products and Services, Technologies, Systems, and Processes

Organizations interested in achieving the FTTM ideal must adopt a philosophy of continuous optimization of products, services, technologies,

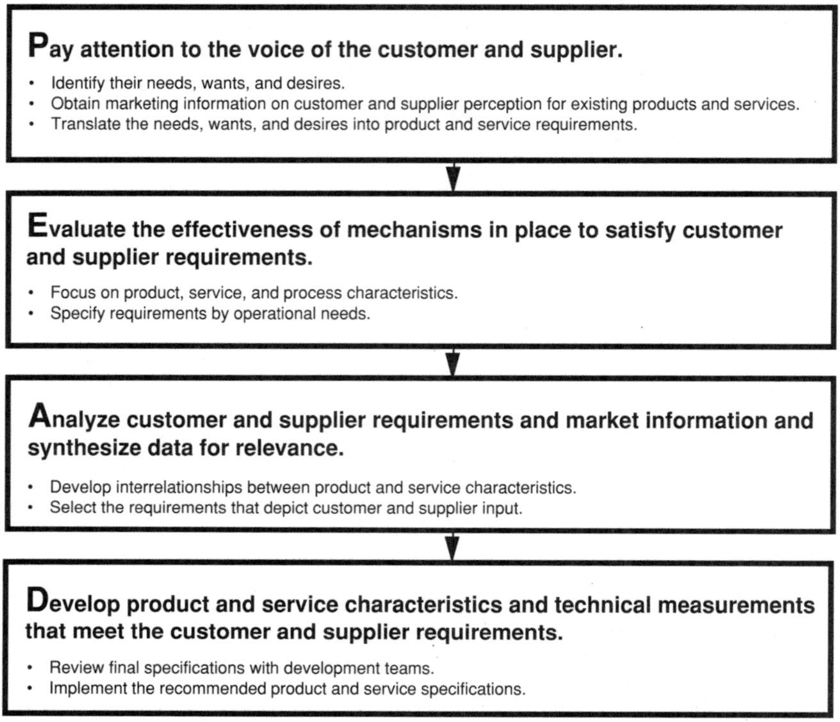

Pay attention to the voice of the customer and supplier.

- Identify their needs, wants, and desires.
- Obtain marketing information on customer and supplier perception for existing products and services.
- Translate the needs, wants, and desires into product and service requirements.

▼

Evaluate the effectiveness of mechanisms in place to satisfy customer and supplier requirements.

- Focus on product, service, and process characteristics.
- Specify requirements by operational needs.

▼

Analyze customer and supplier requirements and market information and synthesize data for relevance.

- Develop interrelationships between product and service characteristics.
- Select the requirements that depict customer and supplier input.

▼

Develop product and service characteristics and technical measurements that meet the customer and supplier requirements.

- Review final specifications with development teams.
- Implement the recommended product and service specifications.

Figure 3.5: The Edosomwan PEAD Model for Capturing Requirements and Needs of the Customer and Supplier

systems, and processes. This philosophy involves continuously enhancing value and excellence. The overall aim of continuous optimization is to minimize the loss imparted by the product or service to the consumer from the time the product or service is developed to customer shipment. This also includes the acceptance of change. Positive changes in product and service strategies will occur through a regular, proactive focus on opportunities for improvement and action on the opportunities. For this activity to occur, employees must understand the required product and service optimization process and techniques. They must be trained in tools and techniques to resolve problems through identification and elimination of root causes. The improvement process should span the entire product and service life cycle. The improvement process should focus on effective ways of integrating product and service development objectives with manufacturing and marketing capabilities. It also involves institutionalizing total performance and improvement in the product and service life cycle from concept to commercialization. Ongoing use of tools and techniques that reduce total cycle time, contribute to improved product and service value, and respond to customer needs is recommended.

Managing the product and service improvement process not only requires pushing the frontiers of technology but also involves the use of continuous improvement, evaluation, control, planning, improvement, and monitoring. The outcome of the improvement process must be benchmarked against that of competitors. This requires the knowledge not only of a specific business unit but of the industry and all competitors in the global marketplace.

Continuous Evaluation and Improvement of FTTM Objectives Using Customer Satisfaction Matrix

At the firm, product, service, and operational unit levels, achievement of FTTM objectives must be continually evaluated to determine whether the final products and services provided meet customer requirements. The evaluation process for final products and services also serves as a means for defining a baseline for product and service performance in the marketplace. With the knowledge gained from the evaluation process, ongoing improvement strategies are employed to achieve future FTTM objectives. The customer is the ultimate judge of the value, price, quality, performance, and usefulness of the products and services. The Edosomwan customer satisfaction matrix (ECSM) shown in Table 3.1 is recommended for evaluating effectiveness of products and services with a focus on FTTM objectives. The ECSM uses the comparative judgment approach (rating scheme for products and services) to evaluate and derive customer satisfaction indices. The ECSM implementation steps are as follows:

Step one: Select the product or service that needs to be evaluated.

Step two: Decide on the customer group size needed to evaluate the product or service selected. A group of 20 or more usually presents a representative data. Small companies with fewer than 20 customers can still use the ECSM even though the sample size may not be statistically significant. The idea is to understand which areas to focus on to improve product and service offerings.

Table 3.1: Edosomwan Customer Satisfaction Matrix (ECSM)

Product	Customer	Measurements/Ratings						Total
		Productivity and performance (PP)	Product quality (PQ)	Delivery schedule (DS)	Competitive price (CP)	Service quality (SQ)	Responsive to customer needs (RN)	
P_1	C_1	5	4	4	3	1	3	
	C_2	2	1	2	2	4	1	
	C_3	3	2	5	1	5	1	
	C_n	2	3	2	1	1	3	
Subtotal		12	10	13	7	11	8	61
P_2	C_1	3	1	4	2	3	1	
	C_2	3	2	1	2	4	1	
	C_3	2	1	3	4	5	1	
	C_4	5	1	3	1	2	2	
	C_n	3	2	2	4	1	1	
Subtotal		16	7	13	13	15	6	70
Total		28	17	26	20	26	14	

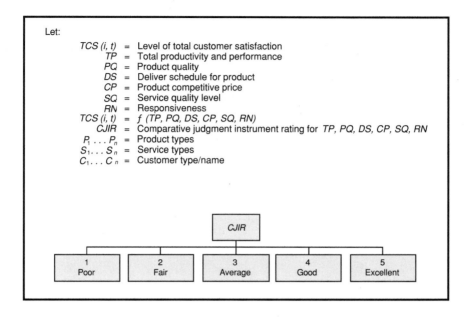

Let:

TCS (i, t) = Level of total customer satisfaction
TP = Total productivity and performance
PQ = Product quality
DS = Deliver schedule for product
CP = Product competitive price
SQ = Service quality level
RN = Responsiveness
TCS (i, t) = f (TP, PQ, DS, CP, SQ, RN)
CJIR = Comparative judgment instrument rating for TP, PQ, DS, CP, SQ, RN
$P_1 \ldots P_n$ = Product types
$S_1 \ldots S_n$ = Service types
$C_1 \ldots C_n$ = Customer type/name

CJIR				
1 Poor	2 Fair	3 Average	4 Good	5 Excellent

Figure 3.6: ECSM Comparative Judgment Definitions and Scale

Step three: Ask the selected customer group to rate the product or service using the criteria and measurements specified in Table 3.1 and Figure 3.6 respectively.

Step four: Tabulate the response by product or source group. This should be done for all six key measurements presented in Table 3.1.

Step five: Develop improvement strategies based on the value of the product and service performance indices obtained.

Step six: Monitor implemented improvement strategies and focus on ongoing assessment of product and service structure, customer base, and organizational performance.

Understanding Customer Requirements

Quality functional deployment (QFD) is a system for translating specific customer wants and needs into specific product and service requirements. QFD can also be viewed as a system for translating customer requirements into appropriate enterprise requirements at each stage from research and product development to engineering, manufacturing,

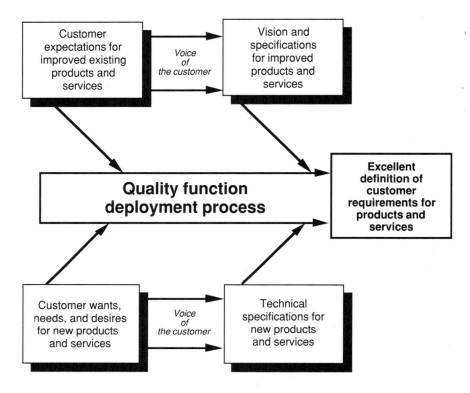

Figure 3.7: Quality Function Deployment and Total Customer Satisfaction

marketing, and distribution. As shown in Figure 3.7, QFD translates the needs, desires, and wants of the customer into requirements that designers and developers can work with to produce products and services. When used properly, QFD provides means for listening to the voice of the customer, translating the needs into product and service characteristics, and prioritizing market requirements. It also provides a means for evaluating key competitive products and services and developing better alternatives.

How to Develop the House of Quality

The eight-step process specified in Figure 3.8 is recommended for developing a matrix called the "house of quality." The completed house of quality should include the customer needs and wants, design functional

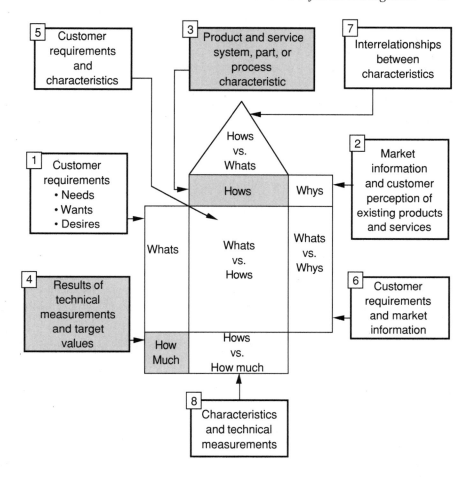

Figure 3.8: Completed House of Quality

characteristics, and depict their relative importance and the interrelationships between all factors. Each step involved in the construction of the house of quality is as follows:

Step one: Listen to the voice of the customer to identify needs, wants, and desires. Translate these into product and service requirements.

Step two: Obtain marketing information and customer perceptions of existing and competing products and services.

Step three: Identify product and service systems, parts, or process characteristics.

Step four: Determine the results of technical measurements and target values.

Step five: Specify key customer requirements and characteristics.

Step six: Analyze customer requirements and market information. Synthesize data for relevance and accuracy.

Step seven: Develop interrelationships between characteristics.

Step eight: Fully define product and service characteristics and technical measurements.

Implementing QFD and Resolving Potential Problems

The following steps are suggested for successful implementation of QFD.

Step one: Incorporate QFD application into the strategic planning process to understand market requirements, identify strengths and weaknesses of existing products and services, and set the strategic direction for new products and services.

Step two: Use QFD to define the relative importance of new products and services. Define the product development, manufacturing, marketing, and distribution processes with detailed specifications and requirements.

Step three: Focus on continuous improvement through careful selection of QFD projects and execution. Make sure that the selected QFD project is related to key business needs. In addition, ensure that the selected project (1) has direct positive impact on internal and external customers, (2) is visible throughout the operational unit, (3) has the endorsement of the overall organization, (4) has a team responsible for project success, (5) is stable, (6) has start and end points defined, (7) has had duplication of effort eliminated, and (8) has QFD problem statement and expected results clearly understood.

Step four: Train everyone in QFD concepts. Encourage use of QFD in capturing the requirements of the customer at every phase of the product or service life cycle.

Top management needs to provide leadership and project team effort to use QFD through the entire business process. In addition, top management should support the implementation of QFD through appropriate setting of business priorities, training middle managers and first-line managers on QFD, insisting that QFD designs are based on facts rather than opinions, communicating the benefits, pitfalls, and the procedures of QFD, and encouraging the use of QFD in all business units.

When implementing QFD, it is easy to mix up requirements—for example, to mix marketing requirements with engineering requirements. Requirement definitions must be analyzed carefully and kept separate. Also, QFD may not work if it is applied too late in the development cycle of a product. QFD must be used early in the product design and development cycle. In addition, the QFD requirement matrices can get too large. To have a simplified QFD matrix, there must be focus on the critical attributes. It is easy to confuse the customer if the questions used to determine the requirements are not stated clearly. Avoid asking customers questions they do not have the technical expertise to understand. It is important to note that QFD can become a meaningless tool if not applied properly to specific projects. Avoid using QFD for every requirement of the business process. Adapt QFD to project needs.

How to Improve the Customer Satisfaction Level

The customer satisfaction model (CSM) shown in Figure 3.9 is based on the premise that total customer satisfaction can be achieved through partnership between supplier, process owner, and customer. Through the application of TQM and QFD, the requirements of the customer, supplier, and process owner are captured and satisfied. The CSM is also based on the principle of continuous process improvement. The continuous improvement process shown in Figure 3.10 consists of four stages.

Stage one—process ownership and accountability: A specific process owner is identified. This person is accountable for the management of the overall process and boundaries. The process owner is also held accountable for the effectiveness and results of the operational work unit. The process owner may elect to manage the entire process through the matrix approach or simply by defining the roles and responsibilities of the supporting function or individuals implementing TQM and QFD throughout the organizations.

Stage two—process assessment, measurement, and evaluation: The customers' needs, wants, desires, and expectations are clearly understood. Specifications for the supplier and process owner are also defined. These requirements are translated into meaningful business products and

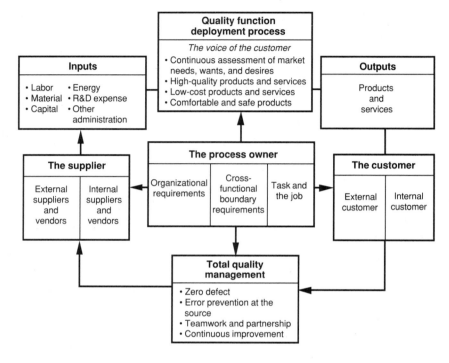

Figure 3.9: The Customer Satisfaction Model

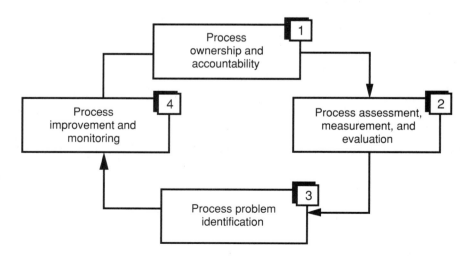

Figure 3.10: Continuous Improvement Process for Customer Satisfaction

services that can be measured, controlled, and improved. Specific measures are then established to control supplier and process owner boundaries to ensure that defect-free products get to the customer.

Stage three—process problem identification: Problems affecting quality, cost, effectiveness, productivity, and total customer satisfaction are identified by operational unit, at the individual level, and by process. These problems are then prioritized using Pareto analysis, which identifies the vital few areas that will yield about 80 percent of the improvement. It also helps the problem analyst identify areas to concentrate resources. This stage should yield a list of key quality and process bottlenecks to be resolved to achieve total customer satisfaction.

Stage four—process improvement and monitoring: Specific improvements are developed and implemented to correct the problems identified in stage three. This stage requires attention to every detail to ensure that internal and external customer problems are resolved. The focus of the process improvement and monitoring stage should be on error prevention and elimination of defects and errors that hinder quality, productivity, and total customer satisfaction.

Enhancing the Customer-Supplier-Process Owner Partnership

Production and service problems can usually be prevented through good communication channels and feedback mechanisms between the supplier, the process owner, and the customer. Adequate partnership results when management and employees are willing to take responsibility for results. Management and employees should also be accountable for all actions and have the desire to satisfy customer requirements. The essential requirements of the supplier, process owner, and customer are presented in Figure 3.11. To enhance this relationship, encourage suppliers and process owners to participate in the quality and process improvement program implementation and provide a mechanism for feedback on product and service quality, pricing policy, new product and service development, and potential problem areas. Conduct a periodic survey to assess customer satisfaction and the essential elements of the supplier-process-owner-customer partnership. Also, provide online communication links between suppliers, process owners, and customers to enable quick identification and resolution of process problems.

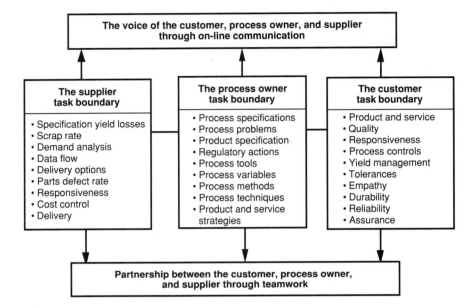

Figure 3.11: Requirements of the Supplier-Process Owner-Customer Partnership

Initiatives for Achieving Total Customer Satisfaction

Personal contact with the customer is one of the most important avenues for maintaining an excellent business relationship. The following initiatives are highly recommended.

- *Executive and management programs:* Assign each executive or manager to a customer account. The executive or manager periodically visits the customer to understand the needs, wants, and requirements. The customer knows who to call when there is a problem; one phone call to one company representative resolves all problems.

- *Accessibility:* Provide expanded hours of service for customer access to the enterprise's operational and service units. Provide a 24-hour toll-free number to a service response center with competent technical personnel.

- *Employee training in customer awareness:* Provide training programs to improve employees' awareness of customer requirements and how to satisfy such needs. The training should focus on communication channels, interpersonnel communications, technical competence, product knowledge, customer buying patterns, customer problems, sales development, service skills, and problem management and resolution. Every employee should be encouraged to identify internal and external customers and develop a strategy for satisfying their requirements.

- *Motivation for total customer satisfaction:* Implement recognition and incentive programs to reward outstanding customer satisfaction initiatives and projects. Publicize such recognition and reward through company newsletters and magazines, bulletin boards, and departmental meetings.

- *Individual action plan:* Every employee should devise an action plan that includes making a commitment to total customer satisfaction, knowing the business of the customer, understanding customer requirements, strengthening actions to improve service to the customer, measuring and improving individual performance, and following up on commitment to the customer.

The survey is the least expensive means of tracking customer satisfaction. Customer satisfaction surveys should be designed to evaluate and identify specific areas for improving performance and effectiveness. Surveys can be designed and used on a monthly, quarterly, semiannual, or annual basis. The measurement process should include, but not be limited to, the following areas: customer service rating, product and service quality, responsiveness to service request, cost competitiveness, failure rates of tools and equipment, number of repeated service calls, installation lead time, late arrival and delivery times, and courtesy and empathy of service personnel.

A good customer tracking system should (1) provide an information data base for customer-related problems on a real-time basis, (2) ensure that customer complaints are communicated quickly across operational units for quick resolution, (3) enhance customer awareness and management of performance problems, (4) compare performance against competitors in the same market, and (5) continuously assess areas for improvement.

Dealing with Customer Complaints

Attracting, serving, and retaining customers is the ultimate business requirement which everyone must strive to achieve. Everyday contacts, along with the things an enterprise does to better serve current customers, help attract future customers. As shown in Figure 3.12, resolving complaints and problems quickly is one of the most important elements to ensure continued customer loyalty and repeat business. Organizations that are best able to understand the requirements of the customer, provide competitive, high-quality products and services, offer total solutions to

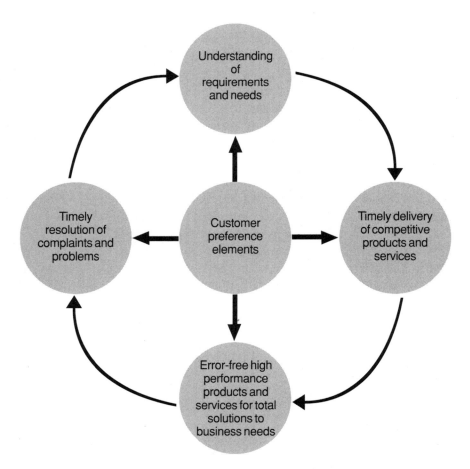

Figure 3.12: Complaint Resolution Model

business needs, and resolve complaints quickly will be able to compete in the global marketplace. Handling customer complaints is probably one of the toughest tasks of anyone providing a product or service in a competitive market. Customer complaints cannot be ignored. They must be handled promptly with the right solutions; otherwise, the customer will go elsewhere.

Complaints can arise from a number of sources.

- *Product and service errors and defects:* Complaints arise from customers disappointed with the quality and performance of products and services. The supplier should expect to hear from an irritated customer with a serious complaint. Pity the customer who buys a $3500 portable computer, takes it home, plugs it in—and nothing happens. Or who invests $28,000 in a car, only to have the transmission go bad immediately after the warranty expires. Or one who gets the wrong cancelled check back from the bank.

- *Poor communication with the end user:* Customers who have been given inappropriate or inadequate information on products and services have the right to complain. What about the customer who buys an item that "requires some assembly" and discovers that instructions are either not available or are written in a style that has more in common with Sanskrit than English? Sympathize with a customer trying to get information about services from a government agency and finding an endless labyrinth of transfers and holds. Pity customers who have to speak with 10 people in an organization before they get the information they want. Lack of communication, slow communication, or inappropriate communication with customers can lead to a number of complaints.

- *People, systems, and procedures:* Poor performance of people, systems, and procedures can lead to customer complaints. Consider a businessperson on a trip to New York City who paid $500 in airfare, had a lousy meal on the plane, and then had to wait four days for his or her luggage to arrive from Japan. Or a shopper in dire need of cash who stops at an automatic teller machine that is "temporarily out of order." Failures in people, systems, and procedures can range from poor product and service attributes that could shut down a business to minor things that can irritate a customer to the point that the next step is to complain, to seek help, or go elsewhere for the product or service. Imagine a customer who was ready to buy a high-priced item from a large department store but needed one bit of information from the salesperson. The salesperson didn't call the potential customer with the information as agreed, and the sale was lost.

Everyone should pay attention to customer complaints. A complaint is always justified from the viewpoint of the person making it, and it is always best to handle customer complaints promptly. Ignoring the complaint or blaming someone else is never the right strategy. The following six guidelines will help those concerned with handling complaints in the interest of total customer satisfaction.

1. Listen to the customer and develop an appreciation for the nature, magnitude, and potential impact of the complaint.

2. Agree that the customer has a valid complaint and apologize on behalf of the organization for any inconvenience. Avoid arguing with the customer or adopting a defensive attitude.

3. Investigate the complaint thoroughly by asking the right questions. Avoid passing the buck to other people when the problem can be solved.

4. Get the facts. Listen carefully to all those who might help provide a solution.

5. If possible, offer an immediate resolution of the problem or inform the customer of the steps necessary to resolve the complaint.

6. If immediate resolution is not possible, get back to the customer promptly when the problem has been resolved. Make the customer feel important. Sympathize with inconveniences and offer solutions that totally resolve the customer complaint. If the customer's demands are unreasonable, convey this to the customer thoughtfully, professionally, and courteously.

It makes good business sense to adopt a "customer-first/the-customer-is-always-right" philosophy. Customers—internal, external, and self-unit—will remain loyal to people and organizations that listen to their requirements and complaints and provide prompt, effective solutions.

Summary

The focus on total customer satisfaction should be integrated into the accepted management process and the enterprise's culture. Everyone must be made aware of internal and external customers. Each individual customer of a product or service is in turn the customer of people working in different jobs in various departments. The key initiatives focus on making quality and total customer satisfaction everyone's mission. Total employee involvement is recommended at all levels of the organization, including customer education, training, and improvement projects. Executives and managers should be put in touch with external customers. A customer-based measure of performance should be included in the reward and recognition mechanism of the enterprise. Periodically require each business unit to develop a strategy for quality excellence and total customer satisfaction and to share customer feedback information with management and employees.

The continuous improvement focus on cost reduction and improved performance and quality can help position an enterprise for long-term profitability and competitiveness. In a competitive world economy, a dissatisfied customer will look for an alternative source of products and services. A satisfied customer will recommend excellent products and services to a friend and help the enterprise increase its market share and profitability.

CHAPTER 4

Problem-Solving Tools and Techniques for Quality and Productivity Management

A market-driven enterprise must focus on ongoing problem identification and resolution, including focus on the supplier, transformation, and customer processes. Problem-solving tools and techniques must be used to improve performance at all levels of the enterprise.

Problem Solving and Completed Staff Work

Problem-solving processes involve the use of rules of reasoning, techniques, tools, attitudes, and adequate information to resolve issues and select the ultimate solution that leads to an explicit goal. Completed staff work means acceptable deliverables (outputs) that are provided for both internal and external customers to obtain a desirable response or decision. The process of achieving completed staff work requires an understanding of the problem and evaluation of the technical accuracy of material. There are three approaches to problem solving. The *behaviorist approach* views problem solving as a relationship between a stimulus (input) and a response (output) without speculating about the intervening process. The *information processing approach* is based on information that accompanies the development of logical programs, such as computer programs. Here, the emphasis is on the process that intervenes between input and output and leads to a desired goal from the initial state. The *block-and-tackle approach* views problem solving as a relationship between cause and effect. Emphasis is placed on identifying the root causes of the problem and their potential effects. Solution strategies are then developed.

Problem solving and completed staff work can be accomplished in the four stages presented in Figure 4.1.

Stage One: Preparation and Planning

In this stage the problem solved determines the objective of the assignment through appropriate communication. The general problem-solving

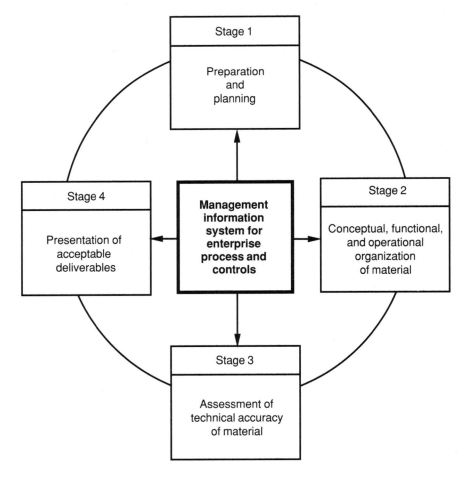

Figure 4.1: Problem Solving and Completed Staff Work

procedure as presented in Figure 4.2 is recommended for identifying and solving problems.

Step one—identify problem and clarify objectives: Specific problems are identified by examining the current mode of operation. Use problem identification tools such as cause-and-effect diagrams, brainstorming techniques, and the error-removal technique. Clearly state the breadth and scope of the problem. Data from process flowcharts, organizational charts, procedures, and policies are usually helpful in specifying the flow of information. Based on the problem(s) identified, formulate specific objectives. These objectives provide a basis for solution and evaluation.

Step two—determine data to be collected: This is usually done through an understanding of the existing methods of accomplishing tasks. The scope of the problem(s) identified in the first step determines how much data is to be collected.

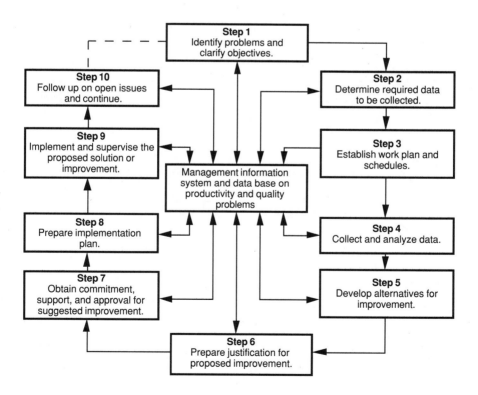

Figure 4.2: General Problem-Solving Procedure

Step three—establish work plan and schedules: The overall problem identified in the first step should be broken down into smaller units by tasks and key processes. This will facilitate the analysis of all segments of the problem. Prepare a plan for addressing the problem with a detailed work schedule, including distribution of activities to be accomplished by individuals and departments that have responsibilities for resolution.

Step four—collect and analyze data: Ensure that the source of data for the problem being addressed is adequate. Carefully observe the activity under analysis to be sure it is thoroughly understood. Analyzing the data requires attention to data classification, verification, and synthesis; checking tables, weights, and figures; and verifying errors.

Step five—develop alternatives for improvement: Reexamine the problem(s) identified in the first step and evaluate the effect of anticipated changes. Collect ideas for solving the problem(s) and make preliminary plans for improvement.

Step six—prepare justification for the proposed improvement: Emphasize cost impact assessment, capital investment, rate of return, intangible benefits, and productivity and quality benefits.

Step seven—obtain approval and support for suggested improvement: Review the proposed improvement with management and employees affected by the change. Revise improvement alternatives based on their input.

Step eight—prepare implementation plan: The implementation plan should include activities, individual responsibilities, and time schedules.

Step nine—implement proposed solution and supervise the installation for effectiveness: The implementation process should include the training of personnel and resource allocation.

Step ten—follow up on open issues: Continue to focus on perpetual improvement. Watch closely for erratic changes, perform periodic evaluation of what has been accomplished, and continue to seek new improvement opportunities.

Stage Two: Conceptual, Functional, Operational Organization of Material

At this stage, the analyst selects the material required according to the objective of the assignment and the problems being addressed. The material is then organized in a logical manner.

Stage Three: Assessment of Technical Accuracy of Material

This stage concerns the thorough assessment and evaluation of completed work. The evaluation should seek answers to the following questions: Does the material introduce the right subject? Does it contain major points and examples that will help to obtain the stated objectives? Does it have continuity? Is it in perspective? Does it examine major and minor points? Has all technical content been checked for accuracy? Are all known questions answered? Does it contain a meaningful conclusion?

Stage Four: Presentation of Acceptable Deliverables

This stage requires understanding the decision points, requirements, process, and deliverables and implementing decision and follow-up.

What to Do When a Problem Is Discovered

When a problem is discovered, it is unproductive to become frustrated and confused. A problem should not be approached from an emotional point of view; rather, a rational approach should be used.

Step one: When there is a problem, stop and look for options. Review the elements of the problem and study their relationships. Next, think about or "sleep on" the problem. Also, discuss the problem and search for a clear understanding of potential root causes. Then prepare a plan for detailed problem analysis.

Step two: Identify the problem(s). Obtain the total picture of the problem being addressed. Avoid quick judgment on causes and solutions. Work with facts, not opinions. The focus should be on processes or actions causing difficulty and on gathering relevant data for addressing key components of the problem.

Step three: Generate lots of ideas on what can be done differently. Write down all ideas. Listen constructively to people's suggestions. Focus on asking the right question and recording relevant answers. Although there is a will to doubt, maintain a sense of objectivity in analyzing ideas. All ideas should be evaluated with the goal of narrowing them down to a workable few.

Step four: Evaluate ideas that focus on the consequences, implementation, and expected benefits. The solution that is implemented must provide a permanent fix to the problem. Solutions should be cost effective and satisfy both the short- and long-term goals. Address the content of the solution, its implementation requirements, and the impact on other areas.

Step five: Implement ideas by using appropriate tools such as a flowchart that contains a work plan with dates for each activity. Implement ideas to correct the problem, evaluate results, and follow up on open issues. The follow-up plan should address key actions that are in place to prevent the problem from recurring.

Mechanisms and Avenues for Resolving Problems

Focus on Teamwork at All Levels

The teamwork approach to problem solving is recommended. Every aspect of the problem can be addressed effectively when both management and employees work on continuous improvement, problem solving, and overall effectiveness. This requires emphasis on innovative approaches to problem solving and constantly finding ways of doing the job better through simplification and method improvement. Teamwork between organizations is also recommended.

Use Experienced Qualified Professionals

In addition to encouraging teamwork at all levels, organization leadership may elect to use experienced managers and technical personnel, consultants, and a task force to resolve productivity and quality issues. The use of individuals, such as experienced technical personnel within the organization, allows those most familiar with current work processes to suggest and implement improvements. The danger in using this approach is that people may not want improvement in the processes within their realm of authority. It also may be difficult to see improvement within a process, given that participants have been used to performing the same functions in a particular way for a long time. Organizations that choose to use this approach must be willing to share gains with their employees and managers that result from new ideas about productivity and quality management.

Use a Task Force

Use a task force when applicable. The task force approach has advantages such as reduced training cost, use of the most competent people, and increased objectivity from members. The task force is often comprised of members from all functions and sectors. The drawback to this approach is that a commitment for follow-up on improvement projects could disappear after the task force is dissolved. The way to avoid this is to assign a specific department or person full accountability for improvement projects provided by the task force.

Use Consultants

This approach brings strong technical proficiency if the consultant is selected properly. The consultant often is neutral about organizational policies since his or her key mission is doing the best job for fair pay. This approach often provides honest and fresh ideas, and it does not require internal training of workers. The result, however, is only as good as the qualifications and experience of the consultant. Insiders often resist consultants. Make a strong effort to seek ideas for improvement. A major drawback to using a consultant is that the burden of commitment and accountability may remain hanging with the senior management unless it is delegated quickly.

Productivity and Quality Assessment Matrix

A major challenge in the satisfaction of customers is providing the right product at the right quantity, at the right time, and at the right price. Unfortunately, two common problems exist at the operational unit and enterprise levels.

First, when the demand for products exceeds the supply, there is pressure to produce more. A typical production manager will push productivity and schedule first. The evaluation procedure ignores quality.

Second, when customer dissatisfaction increases because of poor quality, quality comes first. The need exists for ongoing effective management of the productivity and quality link. Productivity and quality must be managed together to achieve expected levels of output and quality. It is also possible to monitor responsiveness in terms of timeliness as well as quality. Often, if the emphasis is placed on timeliness, quality will suffer; if placed on quality, timeliness will suffer. By monitoring both elements simultaneously, both are given the same emphasis.

The connection between productivity and quality is not taken into account by existing evaluation procedures. The need exists for procedures to balance the requirements of productivity and quality. Figure 4.3 presents the balance of productivity and quality in the business process. Various variables must be managed continuously to provide excellence in productivity and quality. The notion that increases in productivity and improved quality are impossible should be disregarded. Increased productivity and improved quality are possible if one is committed and willing to balance the apparently contradictory sets of goals and objectives.

The productivity and quality assessment matrix (PAQAM) in Figure 4.4 is recommended to industrial managers, decision-makers,

Figure 4.3: Productivity and Quality Balance

and workers interested in balancing expected productivity and quality results. The PAQAM can be used to assess productivity and quality periodically at the individual, task, department, and firm levels. A five-step approach should be followed when using the PAQAM in the work environment.

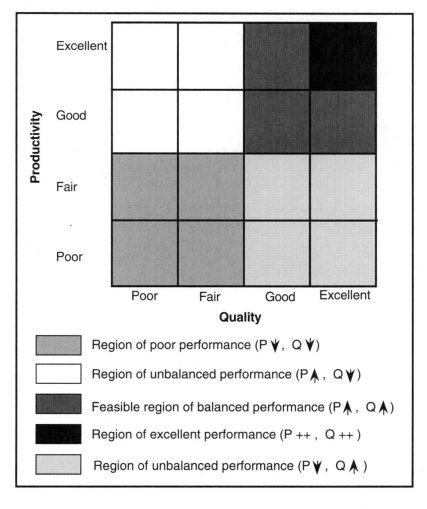

Figure 4.4: Productivity and Quality Assessment Matrix (PAQAM)

Step one: Train everyone in productivity and quality management concepts and techniques. Understand the input and output elements of each task or organization unit, work-flow patterns, procedures, and personnel.

Step two: Develop and implement measurement methods for productivity and quality at the individual, task, and organizational levels. Partial factor, total factor, and total productivity values and indices are recommended. Percent defective, quality index, internal failure costs, external failure costs, appraisal cost, and prevention costs are recommended as adequate measures of quality.

Step three: Classify the productivity and quality measures obtained in step two into categories of poor, fair, good, and excellent. Plot the values obtained in the PAQAM.

Step four: Perform a root cause analysis to determine why a particular performance appears on each region. Implement improvement actions to correct and move a poorly performing individual or task to the region of productivity and quality excellence. To correct poor performance

- Provide ongoing feedback on performance levels.
- Let a poorly performing individual know how he or she is doing on the job.
- Assess any deficiency in skill level required to do the job right and provide the required training to correct the deficiency.
- Initiate on-the-job training and coaching, as needed, to correct deficiencies in skill level.
- Make every effort to match skills to the right job.
- Try job rotation.
- Use experienced, high-performing personnel to train poor performers.
- Let the poorly performing individual accept responsibility for gradual improvement steps to correct low performance levels.
- Reward improvement promptly through appropriate feedback and recognition.

Step five: Follow up periodically on open issues. Train everyone in the organization to use the PAQAM to assess his or her own productivity and quality position. Base productivity and quality rewards on balanced accomplishments.

Using the Histogram to Track Variation

The frequency histogram can be described as a bar graph displaying the frequency distribution of specific processes, items, and devices. This tool provides a valuable means for tracking variation. For instance, it can categorize product defect levels or distribution. A frequency histogram provides the basis for understanding the variation of both production and service scenarios with the visualization to identify opportunity easily with each area (histogram bars) while keeping track of variation. It must be pointed out that frequency histograms do not tell the total sources of variation and do not present a specific pattern over time.

How to Construct a Histogram

Step one: Obtain and record a clear definition of the subject. Define the item(s), device, characteristics, or process which require a frequency histogram to be constructed. For example, a medium-sized company decides to classify the frequency of response time to customer calls when a high-technology insertion machine breaks down. The subject in the example is the customer call's response time for the insertion machine.

Step two: Design, test, and establish a data collection procedure for recording information. If the data collected are to be meaningful, about 20 to 100 observations are recommended. The data collected should represent homogeneous conditions for the process or subject considered. For the auto-insertion customer call's response time example, the 40 observations obtained are presented in Table 4.1.

Step three: Calculate the range of measurement. Circle the largest and smallest number in each group/set and then calculate the range using this formula:

Range value = (highest value – lowest value)

From the example, the range is

$$30 - 1 = 29$$

Step four: Determine histogram width by adding 1 to the range. This is the number required to include all other numerical values. In the example, the width is

$$29 + 1 = 30$$

**Table 4.1: Computer Customer Call's Response Time in Minutes
(40 Observations Used in Construction of Histogram)**

1	4	2	7	8
9	23	16	13	25
16	24	12	13	12
13	17	21	10	19
6	5	30	11	9
15	11	14	27	7
13	17	12	22	16
14	4	6	20	14

Step five: Decide on the number of bars in the histogram. The number of bars is obtained by an approximation technique after careful examination of the total number of observations. The idea is to have all of the observations represented by groups or bars. Table 4.2 presents a guide for determining the number of bars based on the total number of observations.

Table 4.2: Guide for Deriving Histogram Bars

Number of observations	Number of bars
Under 30	3–5
30–50	5–7
50–100	6–10
100–250	7–13
250–1000 (over)	10–25

Step six: Derive class interval with the following formula:

$$\text{Histogram class interval} = \frac{\text{histogram width}}{\text{number of bars}}$$

From the example, the histogram class interval is

$$\frac{30}{6} = 5$$

Step seven: Derive and establish class boundaries by using the following procedure. (1) Assume that the lowest number in the total observations is boundary one. (2) The value of boundary one plus the class width becomes the boundary two value. (3) Continue the successive boundary determination process to determine the total number of boundaries.

Step eight: Tabulate the histogram frequencies. In this step, the various observations are filled into appropriate bars. Table 4.3 shows how the recording process is performed. If the tabulation process is done correctly, the total filled should be equal to the number of observations.

Table 4.3: Frequencies for the Customer Call's Response Time

Bar	Interval	Tallies	Total
1	1–5	/////	5
2	6–10	///// ///	8
3	11–15	///// ///// ///	13
4	16–20	///// //	7
5	21–25	/////	5
6	26–30	//	2
Total		40	40

Step nine: Construct the histogram by devising a chart as shown in Figure 4.5. The y axis should represent the frequency of occurrence while the x axis should represent various intervals. Use an appropriate scale to accommodate the total number of occurrences. By connecting the total points plotted on the graph, the histogram bars are created.

Step ten: Interpret the histogram spread. In this step, the bar graphs are analyzed to provide an understanding of the specific magnitude of each area. In the example presented, most of the customer call frequency occurs between 8 and 13 minutes. This information enables the analyst to see the distribution of the customer call response time as well as specific variations.

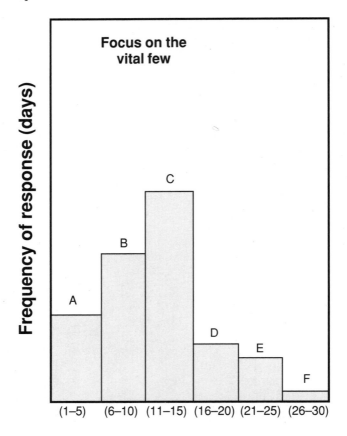

Figure 4.5: Histogram for Auto-Insertion Customer Call's Response Time

Using Pareto Analysis

A Pareto diagram can be described as a graphic representation of identified causes in descending order of magnitude or frequency (see Figure 4.6). The magnitude of concern is usually plotted against the category of concern. The Pareto diagram enables the process improvement analyst to identify key problems, projects, or issues to concentrate on so that resources are allocated to resolve the most important problems. It also identifies the magnitude of the problem that can be eliminated by correcting the most vital issues. It is a valuable tool to use when deciding

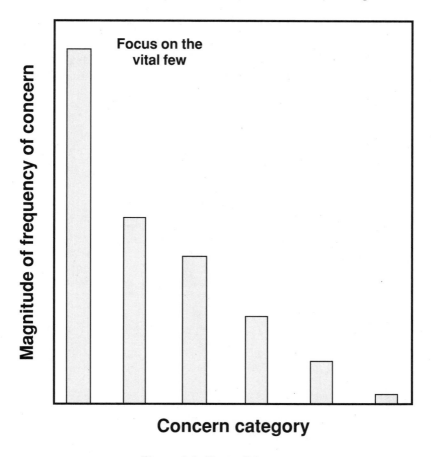

Figure 4.6: Pareto Diagram

which problem to resolve first and what resources should be expanded and approved by management. This tool relies heavily on the ranking process and histogram distribution.

How to Construct a Pareto Diagram

Step one: Specify why a Pareto diagram is required. Provide a clear definition of the items to be ranked, and specify the criteria to be used and the factor. Usually, the motivation of Pareto analysis comes from too many complex problems occurring within an operation unit or a specific process. The Pareto diagram is then used to categorize the problems in their order of magnitude. For example, a computer manufacturer wanted to understand the repair and analysis cost associated with specific types of computer products. Pareto analysis technique provided an understanding of the magnitude of this problem.

Step two: Perform data collection and record by item. Collect and record the number of occurrences of each problem and the associated magnitude in weight, cost, or time. For the computer products example, the repair and analysis cost of each type of computer is presented in Table 4.4.

Table 4.4: **Repair and Analysis Cost for Computer Products**

Computer types	Defect occurrence (total numbers)	Average cost per occurrence ($)	Total repair cost per computer type ($)
C1	15	20	300
C2	18	40	720
C3	20	10	200
C4	14	5	70
C5	10	10	100
C6	5	25	125
Total	82		1515

Step three: Calculate percentages for each item and rank order. The percentages for each item and the total cumulative percentages for all items are calculated as follows:

$$\text{Item \%} = \frac{\text{each items (weight or value)}}{\text{total items (weight or value)}} \times 100$$

Example for computer type C2

$$\text{Item \%} = \frac{}{1515} \times 100\% = 47.5\%$$

$$\text{Cumulative \%} = (\text{each item \%} + \text{previous cumulative \%})$$

For the computer example, the product and cumulative percentages are presented in Table 4.5.

Table 4.5: Product and Cumulative Costs for Computer Products

Computer types	Repair and analysis cost ($)	Computer products (%)	Cumulative (%)
C1	300	19.8	67.3
C2	720	47.5	47.5
C3	200	13.2	80.5
C4	70	4.6	100.0
C5	100	6.6	95.4
C6	125	8.3	88.8
Total		100	

Step four: Construct graph axes and plot bars and cumulative percentage line. Based on the values of items obtained in step three, the Pareto diagram is constructed. For the computer example, the Pareto diagram is presented in Figure 4.7.

Constructing a Fishbone (Cause-and-Effect) Diagram

The fishbone or cause-and-effect diagram shown in Figure 4.8 helps to relate the elements of a process. It relates possible causes to specific effects. All variation levels are identified by examining all the possible causes. All the possible causes that add to the variation level of the resulting effects are identified using a brainstorming approach. The cause-and-effect diagram provides a method of involving all the people and factors in the service or manufacturing process to see how various factors come together to make up the total performance.

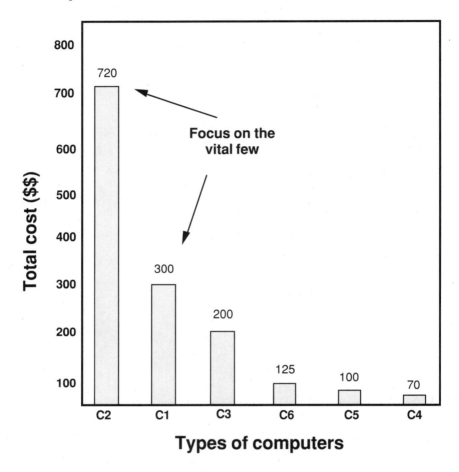

Figure 4.7: Example of Diagram for Computer Products

The steps for constructing a fishbone diagram and implementing recommended solution strategies are as follows:

Step one: Perform a thorough analysis of the production or service operation work unit and define the reason for using the fishbone diagram.

Step two: Initiate meetings involving all parties known to be affected by the problem.

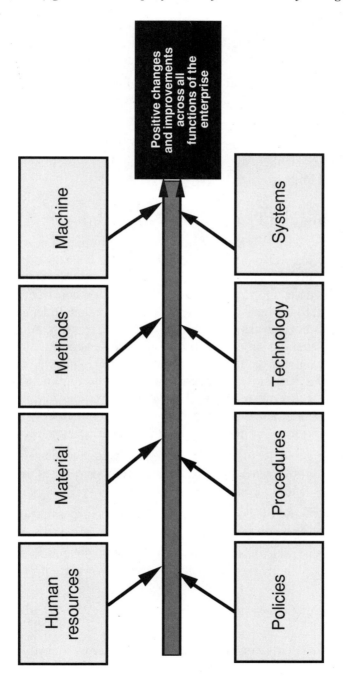

Figure 4.8: Fishbone or Cause-and-Effect Diagram

Step three: Use the brainstorming or nominal group technique to identify all possible causes of the specific problem and identify potential effects on quality, performance, productivity, and total customer satisfaction.

Step four: Pinpoint the main causes of the problem. Identify the key contributor (machine, material, methods, technology systems, people, policies, or procedures).

Step five: Develop alternative solutions for the problem.

Step six: Implement the solution and follow up with continuous corrective action and improvement.

Flowcharting and Process Analysis Technique

A flowchart shown in Figure 4.9 provides an example of how various factors may be interrelated in an assembly process. It provides the basis for understanding the standard process procedures, the relationships between the people, and the work to be done. When constructed accurately and analyzed properly, a flowchart can help users understand and identify process bottlenecks such as delays, excessive transportation, waiting time, and queuing time. It also identifies key customers, suppliers, and process owners by operational work unit; performance level; quality level; and productivity at each process point. Flowcharting can also identify sources of errors, waste, non–value-added operations, and introduction steps for new products and services.

The following steps are recommended for constructing a flowchart.

Step one: Understand the process and the relationship between all process parameters (manpower, machine, materials, methods, procedures, technology, systems, and policies).

Step two: Understand the flowchart process symbols (process, transportation, delays, and decision points).

Step three: Construct the flowchart starting with the first activity or event. Connect all activities or processes using arrows in chronological order.

Step four: Identify the key problems by reviewing every step and element specified.

Step five: Develop a solution strategy for problems, identifying and implementing corrective actions for continuous improvement.

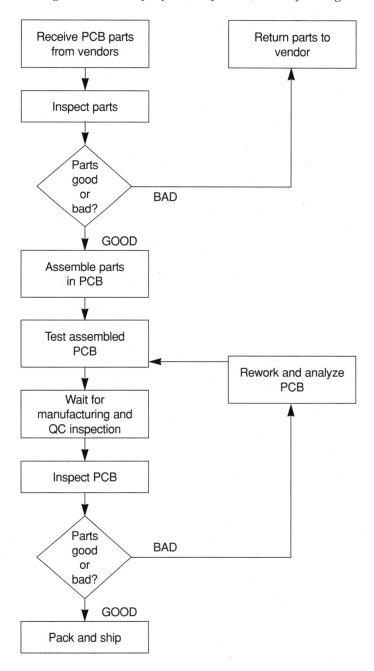

Figure 4.9: Flowchart of Printed Circuit Board (PCB) Assembly Process

Productivity and Quality Evaluation Procedure

The productivity and quality evaluation procedure (PAQEP) is developed to assist industrial managers and production and quality assurance personnel in making a fair trade-off between quality and productivity requirements. The terms of productivity and quality used for PAQEP are as follows:

Quality: "fitness for use," "conformance to specification;" measured as defect per unit

Total productivity: the ratio of total output to all input factors

Total factor productivity: the ratio of total output to the sum of associated labor and capital (factor) inputs

Partial productivity: the ratio of total output to one class of input

PAQEP is also based on the following assumptions:

- Quality and productivity standards do exist at the operational unit level.
- The quality focus is on error prevention and defect elimination.
- The productivity focus is on effective utilization of all resources to produce useful output.

The mathematical expressions for PAQEP are as follows:

Let

$QPR\ (i,\ t)$ = Quality and Productivity Rating for task i in period t

$QF\ (i,\ t)$ = Quality Factor weight (a constant) for task i in period t

$QM\ (i,\ t)$ = Quality measure in percent for task i in period t

$PM\ (i,\ t)$ = Productivity measure in percent for task i in period

$PF\ (i,\ t)$ = Constant factor for other variables affecting the balance between productivity and quality task i in period t

$VF\ (i,\ t)$ = Constant factor for other variables affecting the balance between productivity and quality for task i in period t

$RT\ (i,\ t)$ = Ranking of task i in period t, based on $QPRit$ values

$AP\ (i,\ t)$ = Adjusted productivity in percent for task i in period t

$ER\ (i,\ t)$ = Error rate in percent for task i in period t

$EF\ (i,\ t)$ = Error rate factor (constant) for task i in period t

Where

$$i = 1, 2 \ldots n, \qquad t = 1, 2, 3 \ldots m$$

$EF\ (i,\ t) = 1$ for low error rate

$EF\ (i,\ t) = 2$ for medium error rate

$EF\ (i,\ t) = 4$ for high error rate

$$QF\ (i,\ t) + PF\ (i,\ t) + VF\ (i,\ t) = 1 \ \ldots\ldots\ldots\ldots\ldots\ldots\ldots\ldots\ldots(1)$$

$$QM\ (i,\ t)[VF\ (i,\ t)] + [100 - PM\ (i,\ t)][VF\ (i,\ t)] \ldots\ldots\ldots\ldots(2)$$

$$ERit = PM\ (i,\ t) - QMit \ldots\ldots\ldots\ldots\ldots\ldots\ldots\ldots\ldots\ldots\ldots(3)$$

$$APit = PM\ (i,\ t) - [ER\ (i,\ t) \times EF\ (i,\ t)] \ldots\ldots\ldots\ldots\ldots\ldots(4)$$

PAQEP Case Study

The production manager in a computer manufacturing plant had the data presented in Table 4.6 on quality and productivity performance for computer assembly tasks during one month. The production manager is interested in evaluating the quality and productivity rating and the ranking for each task.

Table 4.6: Quality and Productivity Performance Data on Computer Assembly Tasks

Task	% Quality [QM (i, t)]	Quality constant factor [QF (i, t)]	Productivity [PM (i, t)]	Productivity constant factor [FF (i, t)]	Constant factor for other variables [VF (i, t)]
Component ASM (T1)	90	0.4	98	0.4	0.2
Sub-ASM (T2)	96	0.4	100	0.4	0.2
Pack and Ship (T3)	99	0.4	105	0.4	0.2

As shown in Table 4.6, quality and productivity are given equal emphasis. When the costs of poor quality are very high, quality should receive more emphasis. The weight assigned to quality should therefore be higher than that assigned to productivity. The three factors—0.4, 0.4, and 0.2—must add up to 1.0 to keep the ratings close to 100. Any slight change in the constant weighing factors for quality, productivity, and other variables will drastically change the ranking for each task. It is very important that the constant factors (that is, the relative emphasis) be based on experience with production runs of 30 or more. Users of the PAQEP procedure must be aware of the chosen values for constant factors. One of the common problems in using this evaluation procedure is the difficulty involved in obtaining adequate quality and productivity data. Also, production managers have the tendency to push productivity when there is pressure to satisfy customer demands. When this happens, quality is sacrificed. As the number of products and tasks increases, data manipulation and tracking can become cumbersome. This problem can be resolved by using a computer-assisted data collection system. Ranking values shown in Tables 4.7 and 4.8 can be used to prioritize tasks for improvement opportunity in quality and productivity.

Table 4.7: Calculation and Ranking of Performance Data of Table 4.6

Task	Quality and productivity rating calculation $[QPR (i, t)]$	Result	Ranking
T1	$[90 \times 0.4]+[98 \times 0.4]+[(100 - 90)(0.2)]+[(100 - 98)(0.2)]$	77.6	3
T2	$[96 \times 0.4]+[100 \times 0.4]+[(100 - 96)(0.2)]+[(100 - 100)(0.2)]$	79.2	2
T3	$[99 \times 0.4]+[105 \times 0.4]+[(100 - 99)(0.2)]+[(100 - 105)(0.2)]$	80.8	1

Table 4.8: Percentage Error and Productivity for Computer Assembly Task Error

Task	% Error calculation	% Error	Adjusted productivity calculation $AP (i, t) = P_m (i, t) - [ER (i, t) - EF (i, t)]$	Adjusted productivity %
T1	$[98 - 90]$	2	$98 - [1.5 \times 2]$	95
T2	$[100 - 96]$	4	$98 - [1.5 \times 2]$	94
T3	$[105 - 99]$	6	$105 - [1.5 \times 6]$	96

[Rate constant factor assumed as 1.5 (medium error rate value)]

The potential degree of success depends on how well employees and management choose to operate a formal productivity and quality program. Management must be willing to commit investment and resources to productivity and quality programs that have both short-term and long-term payoff. Perhaps the proper measure of a balanced productivity and quality program is the degree to which everyone in the organization is willing to take responsibility for and pride in the final work output that goes to the customer.

Nominal Group Technique

The nominal group technique (NGT) is a proactive search process that involves a group approach to identifying specific problems and issues or providing solutions to problems previously identified. It is a method of generating ideas, recording those ideas, and prioritizing them to move toward consensus decisions. NGT can be especially useful when resolving complex problems, or when a group is under time pressure, or to avoid potential conflicts associated with discussing and prioritizing sensitive issues. An example using NGT appears in Figure 4.10. The steps are described here.

Step one—idea generation process: The leader of the group presents the purpose of the meeting, such as to generate ideas for resolving a specific productivity and quality problem. The ground rules for proactive group participation are provided, group members individually record ideas on paper without comment.

Step two—reporting of ideas: Two methods are commonly used. (1) If the ideas are sensitive or if there are many participants or ideas, the facilitator collects the ideas and records them individually and anonymously for the group. (2) Each person can present his or her ideas in turn. No evaluation or prejudgment is allowed by other team members while the facilitator records the ideas.

Step three—clarification and discussion of ideas: Once all ideas have been recorded, each one is discussed to ensure accurate interpretation, clarify misunderstandings, and combine duplicate ideas.

Step four—ranking of ideas: Ideas are prioritized by each participant. There are many methods for ranking, the most common being simple voting or weighted voting and Pareto prioritization. The goal of this step is to reach a consensus on the ideas of greatest interest.

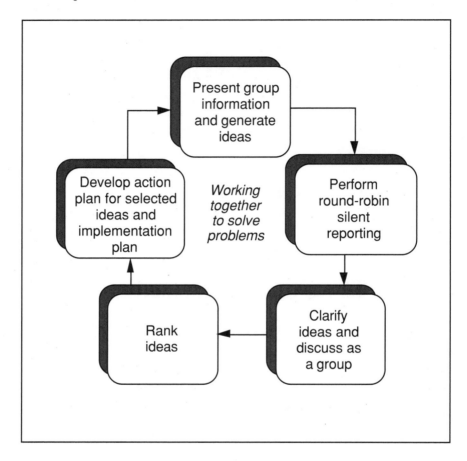

Figure 4.10: Steps for Conducting Nominal Group Technique

Step five—implementation: Once an idea is selected for recommendation or implementation, the group develops an implementation plan and establishes a time line of expected results.

Force Field Analysis

The force field analysis (FFA) technique is a graphic means of understanding the positive and negative forces that prevent goal achievement. FFA assumes that an individual or group can recognize things that will either increase or decrease the likelihood of achieving a goal. This tool also focuses on early identification of the stepping-stones and roadblocks associated with a problem. This permits a clear focus on a plan of action that will support goal attainment.

FFA should be used to plan the strategy for resolving a problem; collect data for problem analysis; understand the negative and positive influences of a problem; generate and weight alternative solutions; and select the most effective solution strategy for implementation. The following steps are recommended for the application of FFA.

Step one: Determine the goal and define it accurately.

Step two: Using a large notepad (or a blackboard), draw a broken vertical line down the right side, a solid vertical line down the center, and a horizontal line across the top of the two vertical lines, as shown in Figure 4.11. The broken line symbolizes the desired state and the solid line symbolizes the current state. The example in Figure 4.11 describes a "current computer product" as the current state and a "new computer product" as the future or desired state. This notepad serves as the recording instrument.

Step three: Brainstorm for items that will help to influence movement from the current situation toward the goal. The example in Figure 4.11 lists three items. Record the items to the left of the "current computer product" line and draw a process arrow from the item to the line. The length of the arrow should be used to approximate the degree of impact that item will have on attaining the goal.

Step four: Brainstorm for items that will detract from the process of changing the current situation. Record these items to the right of the "current computer product" line and draw an arrow to it. The length of the process arrow should represent the impact of that item in detracting from goal achievement.

Step five: Discuss and record the strategy, goals, and a realistic time line for reducing or eliminating each negative force or increasing the positive to move toward the desired state.

Summary

There are many reasons why an enterprise should focus on continuous problem solving and resolution. Problem solving and resolution enables the work processes to be improved, which leads to quality output that satisfies customer requirements. Problem identification can lead to root

Step 1

New product idea!

Goal: High-quality, low-cost computer
that meets customer specifications

Step 2

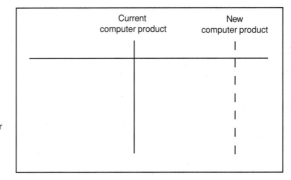

Step 3

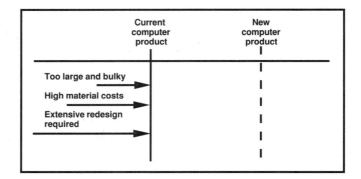

Step 4

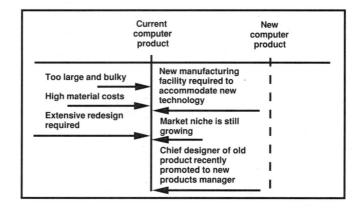

Figure 4.11: Force Field Analysis Example

causes of eroding profit margins, low customer satisfaction, and poor product and service strategy. Resolving problems also facilitates teamwork among suppliers, process owners, and customers. No enterprise can improve without ongoing focus on the application of the right tools to solve problems.

Continuous improvement tools and techniques should be used for total quality and productivity management. Productivity and quality requirements should be managed together. The people and functions that produce the final output for the organization must be willing to work together. Effective teamwork can help ensure that both the production manager and the quality manager meet the objective of providing a quality product to the customer. Productivity and quality requirements and expected output should be balanced at the individual, task, department, and organizational level.

The success of an enterprise in introducing a new product or service promptly to the market depends on organized use of the model and tools presented in this chapter. The teamwork approach to building quality into products and services is recommended.

CHAPTER 5

Error Prevention and Cost of Quality Management

The customer deserves error-free and defect-free work output. The best strategy for achieving excellence is through emphasis on prevention of errors and defects. Encourage the philosophy to build quality into the product at the source. Preventing errors of all kinds can help control quality costs.

Quality errors can be defined as obstacles, mistakes, and delays in performance which influence product and service quality, productivity, efficiency, and organizational effectiveness.

Sources and Types of Quality Errors

Decision-Oriented Quality Errors

Decision-oriented quality errors arise from exercising bad judgment and making decisions that hurt the quality of work output and performance. Decision-oriented quality errors are not limited to managers and supervisors; these errors occur at all levels of the organization. These errors can be corrected by using adequate supporting data as the basis for making decisions. Training in decision-making tools and techniques, communication procedures, and decision impact analysis procedures is also recommended.

Environment-Oriented Quality Errors

Quality errors caused by environmental influence are related to product specifications required by law or imposed by natural limitations. These errors are usually corrected through adjustment of processes related to environmental regulations. These errors cause enormous frustration at lower levels of the enterprise because of the time involved in correcting them. The strategy for prevention should include a thorough analysis of environmental regulations, laws, procedures, and limitations prior to establishing a production or service process.

Policy and Procedure Quality Errors

These errors are caused by operating policies and procedures set by management. These can be corrected by training people on how to follow procedures. Management plays a key role in correcting these types of errors. Usually, policies and procedures have to be rewritten or reevaluated for clarity. General quality problems result from errors made because of deviation from correct procedure or deviation from procedure verification and auditing. Continuous enforcement of correct procedures is recommended for preventing these types of errors.

Technique and Method Quality Errors

These errors are caused by the use of poor methods or techniques for performing work, lack of skills to perform required work activity, poor process design, and inadequate work-flow patterns. These types of errors can be prevented by providing adequate tools and developing proper processes and techniques. Emphasis on training and continuous education for knowledge enhancement is highly recommended.

Inadvertent Quality Errors

These quality errors are caused by human weakness and inattention to detail. Types of error range from forgetfulness to omission of data. These errors are difficult for workers to avoid, especially when they perform repetitive tasks requiring large stretches of concentration. Inadvertent quality errors can be corrected through training in concentration, job rotations, rest breaks, job redesign, and job enrichment.

Design and Planning Quality Errors

These errors are caused by poor design and planning and also by ignorance of operations. They can be corrected by using proper planning tools, management techniques, and time management, and by training personnel in planning techniques.

Technology-Oriented Quality Errors

These quality errors are caused when technology or systems malfunction. These errors can be corrected by preventive maintenance of technology and systems and by improving the reliability of systems and technology.

Values and Data Quality Errors

Values and data quality errors are caused by incorrect application of language and numbers. Manual-intensive processes also increase the chances of mistakes in data manipulation and value interpretation. These errors are usually corrected through training and automation. Data directories can also be used as corrective means.

Process Problem Complexity Quality Errors

Process problem complexity quality errors occur when the design of production and service processes is too complex for human control. These errors can be eliminated by keeping the process design simple. The simpler the process, the easier it is for humans to control, and hence fewer process technical problems occur.

How to Prevent Quality Errors and Defects

Attitude Orientation and Training

This approach focuses on correcting poor attitudes that lead to error. At the individual level, attitudes that lead to error are identified and discussed. Encourage an attitude of care, empathy, concern, alertness, awareness, and pride in excellent output. Stress the need for quality at the source of production and service. Encourage employees to identify problem areas that affect their decision latitude, attitude toward work, and quality of output. Encourage and implement employee-oriented solutions for correcting such problems. Make everyone aware that quality errors may easily turn a paying customer away. Encourage the attitude that seeks to do the job right the first time. Training plays a vital role in supplying the necessary knowledge to do the job right. Organize training in existing and new techniques to prevent errors. On-the-job training, coaching by peers and supervisors, classroom training, and workshops are highly recommended. The strategy is to hire the right person with the right attitude and to provide the required training to get the job done right the first time.

Process Control

Characterization and control of production and service processes supports defect prevention and elimination. This approach focuses on understanding the sources and pattern of variation and performance characteristics of personnel, tools, machines, materials, methods, and processes. Techniques such as statistical process control, design of experiment, work simplification, process flow analysis, and improvement can control known variations and potential quality errors. A good process control system enables self-verification for accuracy and completeness. There is no need for multiple inspection. Identify key process parameters with potential error sources and error correction approaches. This usually requires good process measurement techniques and mechanisms for implementing corrective actions.

Recognition and Reward

This approach focuses on recognizing and rewarding individual and group efforts that lead to error elimination and quality improvement. Recognition and reward are offered for discovering and eliminating production and service errors and inconsistencies. Process control, innovative quality, and productivity improvement are also rewarded.

Verification Methods

The verification approach to error prevention focuses on inspection, audit, review, and verification of work output during and after completion. This is an expensive approach for preventing quality errors. Some of the methods used for verification are multiple inspection, self-verification and review, supervisory review, computerized verification, data verification, and communication verification. Test processes are also methods of verification. Most methods other than self-verification add no value to the product or service, and sometimes errors can be created during verification and inspection. If used correctly, the approach can prevent quality errors.

Operating Methods

This approach emphasizes quality error prevention through correct methods of doing work at individual and group levels. Some of the methods include group problem solving and error analysis; process analysis technique; establishing clear and complete communication channels, clear lines of responsibility and authority, and clear procedures; and individual daily error analysis, control, and improvement.

The Quality Error Prevention Model

The quality error prevention model and error correction steps shown in Figures 5.1 and 5.2 are recommended for error prevention at the source of production and service. The essentials of the model are presented in the following steps.

Step one: Identify sources of quality errors by review process, performance data, skill-base analysis, study of potential problem cause and effect, and interviews with process owner.

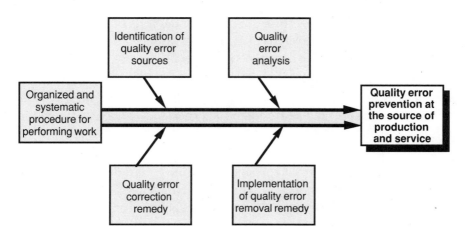

Figure 5.1: Quality Error Prevention Model

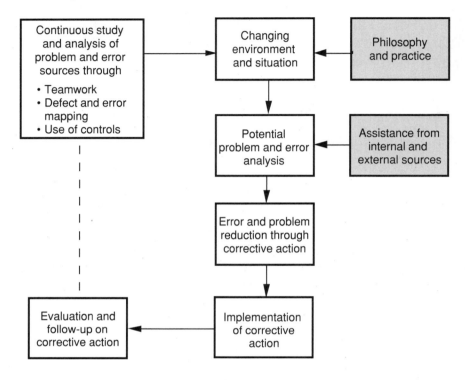

Figure 5.2: Error Correction Steps

Step two: Analyze quality errors to determine the facts of error causation after careful review and analysis of data, methods, procedures and operation, types and locations of error, person responsible, tools, and machine.

Step three: Brainstorm for alternative solutions and error correction remedies. Select the error correction remedy that will eliminate all effects and impact. Use sound reasoning and experience to select the right remedy.

Step four: Implement the quality error correction remedy, and monitor results. The application of the selected remedy should address both immediate and long-term problems. Monitoring provides a feedback mechanism on whether or not the errors are corrected and improvement is achieved. The monitoring work may dictate or highlight additional areas for improvement.

Step five: Focus on continuous improvement through organized and systematic ways of performing work. The prevention process for quality errors is never-ending. At the individual and group levels, encourage attention to clean desks and work environments. An organized and systematic approach to problem solving and complete staff work is highly recommended.

Using the Matrix Analysis Technique for Quality and Productivity Errors

Production and service errors can usually be traced to seven sources: (1) machines, (2) materials, (3) human resources, (4) processes, (5) methods, (6) systems, and (7) technology. The matrix analysis technique is useful in assessing the magnitude of errors by various source points. Error types are classified by source point. The process-error matrix shows the magnitude of each error type by process, while the task-error matrix shows the magnitude of each error type by task. An example of the process-error matrix is presented in Table 5.1. Once the magnitude of errors is determined using the matrix analysis technique, the causes of error are determined and corrective actions are implemented to correct the problems.

Table 5.1: Process-Error Matrix for Electronic Manufacturing

Error type	Process			
	P1 Component assembly	P2 Cover assembly	P3 Product test	P4
Defective components E1	2	4	6	1
Missing components E2	1	1	2	1
Loose screws E3	3	0	2	2
Wrong labels E4	1	1	0	5
Total error by process ET	7	6	10	9

Quality Error Removal Technique

Teamwork in operational work units, departments, and functional areas is essential for error prevention. Everyone's knowledge and problem-solving skills are essential in resolving quality and productivity errors in the complex relationships between input-process-output of production and service systems. The Edosomwan quality error removal (QER) technique (shown in Figure 5.3) is used for problem solving and resolution at the source of production and service. The QER technique provides organized guidelines and principles for a group of workers who decide to work together. Errors can be presented and resolved through focus on the following.

Break down organizational goals into specific small tasks at the operational unit level. Apply continuous effort to improve productivity and

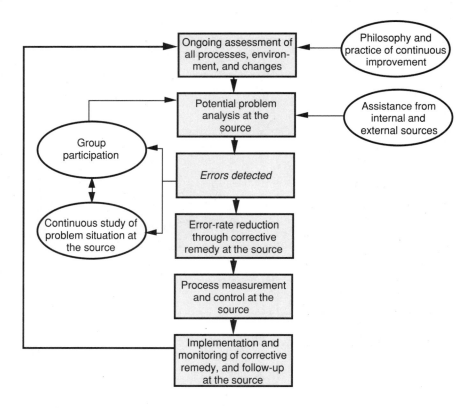

Figure 5.3: Quality Error Removal Model

quality within each work unit. Teach workers basic job skills and cross train for multiple skills. Both employees and management will be convinced that productivity and quality improvement is possible in an organization and within each task unit once everyone involved understands how the job should be performed to deliver a good product. Everyone also understands the nature of the product or service being delivered. Two types of training are encouraged: formal training through a company educational program or an outside institution, and training by peers.

Encourage decision making and problem solving at the source of production or service. At the operational level, QER teams select their own problems on which to focus and decide how to attack bottleneck issues that prevent productivity and quality improvement. The team identifies problems over which there is control. All members of the team freely contribute ideas and reach a consensus on the best possible solution. The brainstorming technique is highly encouraged. Use the following steps to understand the cause and effect of a key problem: define the problem precisely; draw a flow diagram and label all categories of problems; brainstorm to identify the root cause of the problem; use a Pareto diagram to select a problem on which to focus; obtain consensus on a solution; implement the solution; and follow up on issues.

Encourage productivity and quality improvement at the source of production or service. Each product or service is inspected at the source. Members of the QER team perform inspection of their own work. Quality and productivity errors are resolved by joint effort among team members. Teams have checkpoints to review all outgoing finished products. Any member of the team can call for group help to reach a consensus on key problems quickly. Feedback mechanisms between each quality circle (QC) team member are immediate. Team members are viewed as teachers and error-correction masters.

Encourage the QC team characteristics: establish a forum for sharing ideas; maintain a high level of communication among team members, and encourage everyone to participate with enthusiasm; ensure that supervisors or managers support the team to resolve problems when called upon; and make sure rewards and recognition are shared among team members. All members of the team should clearly understand and agree on goals.

Provide clear definitions of roles and responsibilities to the QC team. The recommended definitions of roles and responsibilities are as follows:

- *Teacher:* The person who trains team members in skills needed to perform the task. Everyone on the QC team is a teacher at one stage or another.

- *Team leader:* The person who leads the team in resolving a key problem. The team leader is chosen by voluntary means. Each member of the QC team inherits leadership on a rotational basis.

- *Team members:* A group of people who participate in the problem-solving and resolution process. The team meets regularly at a specified time and location to provide a consensus that resolves problems related to its tasks.

- *Facilitator:* A team member who records the team's progress, keeps records of the agenda, and assists the team leader in accomplishing the team's stated objectives.

- *Team correction master:* Any member of the team who identifies a quality error in the output produced by other team members. Such a member ensures that the error is corrected at the source of production or service. All team members participate in a random and revolving inspection process to help detect quality errors.

- *Team presentations:* Presentations to management of the team's accomplishments. Presentations are rotated among team members. The presenter introduces team members. The agenda and the presentation package are prepared by all members of the team. The following QER implementation methodology is recommended.

Step one: Allow the formation of the QC team to revolve by itself at any level.

Step two: Allow a specific QC team formed for a specific problem to define its own objectives, agenda, meeting times, procedures, and training processes. Avoid excessive supervisory and management intervention at this point.

Step three: Provide the required training for the QC team as it relates to specific tasks and decision-making processes.

Step four: Train the QC team on QER guidelines and principles, including problem-solving approaches.

Step five: Have the QC team generates a list of potential problems that require resolution.

Step six: Ensure that the QC team uses Pareto analysis and cause-and-effect diagrams to select focus problem(s).

Step seven: Recommend that the nominal group technique be used as the QC team brainstorms on the possible root causes of the problems.

Step eight: Have the QC team analyze problem root causes, develop possible solutions, and reach consensus on a solution implementation strategy.

Step nine: Provide assistance, as needed, as the QC team prepares progress evaluation procedure and implements new idea(s) to resolve problem.

Step ten: Watch as the QC team presents progress to management periodically, obtains approvals for resources required, and specifies action items and expected results for implemented action. The team should continue to hold regular sessions to follow up on improvement and look for new areas of opportunity. The team dissolves when its services are no longer required or when there is no meaningful problem for it to resolve.

What Are Quality Costs?

Quality costs identify areas of opportunities to reduce cost, improve productivity, and increase total customer satisfaction. Quality cost systems aid in setting priorities for quality improvement projects, studying cost trends to reallocate resources, focusing multistep operations, measuring performance, and balancing efforts in reducing variation in design. Quality costs can estimate the amount of money involved in poor quality and the amount spent trying to measure and prevent it. This is the total quality cost concept. Realizing how large this amount is, a company is motivated into doing something about it. Total quality costs of as much as 25 percent of sales are not unusual before quality cost improvement programs are implemented.

Quality cost can also help choose improvement projects based on projected return on investment. Other areas of application include measures of quality performance; data for annual and quality improvement plans; and measures of the effect of the quality component in on-the-job training processes.

Types of Quality Costs

Prevention Costs

Prevention costs are associated with designing, implementing, and maintaining a quality system capable of anticipating and preventing quality problems before they generate avoidable costs. This category includes all costs of design and manufacturing efforts to prevent nonconformance. Typically, these include the costs of training, new products' review, burn in, problem solving and consulting, quality planning, quality control system, and user, supplier, and customer testing of the quality control system.

Appraisal Costs

Appraisal costs are incurred to detect errors. These costs are associated with measuring, evaluating, or auditing products, processes, components, and purchased materials to assure conformance to quality standards and performance specifications. They include the costs of inspection and testing of incoming parts or materials, equipment maintenance for accuracy and reliability, verification of process performance, and materials and services consumed in destructive test cycles.

Internal Failure Costs

Internal failure costs are associated with products, components, and materials that fail to meet quality requirements when such failure is discovered prior to delivery of the product to the customer. Internal failure costs can also be defined as costs incurred in correcting errors before delivery of the product. Such costs typically include failure analysis, rework and repairs, wasted tools and equipment, yield losses, retesting of products after rework, and scrap control.

External Failure Costs

External failure costs are incurred in correcting errors after delivery of the product to the customer. These costs are generated by defective products or services which fail to satisfy the customer requirements and do not conform to specifications. Such costs include warranty charges, liability costs, penalties, interest payments due to late deliveries of products and services, error investigation charges, transportation to and from the customer site, and indirect costs.

Summary

Once the cost of quality has been determined, obtain the cost of quality and design improvement projects to achieve cost reduction. Focus on areas that require more definitive analysis of the data to pinpoint areas of greatest excess cost. Break down cost by functional areas. Analyze available data and pinpoint problem areas, and brainstorm for alternative solutions. Select and implement the solution that reduces or eliminates the quality cost identified.

Understanding the cost of quality helps in understanding the amount of money involved in poor quality. It also helps in the choice of quality cost improvement projects.

The emphasis in quality assurance should be on error and defect prevention. Defect identification through inspection is very costly. Defect and error prevention is more cost effective than inspection and detection. Quality starts with the right attitude and is enhanced by adequate skills, tools, techniques, and technologies.

_____ CHAPTER 6 _____

Understanding and
Controlling Variation

Variation is a natural enemy that is found in all stages of product life cycle, including design and development, manufacturing, service, and supplier processes. Controlling process variation is key to quality and productivity improvement.

Variation (normal or abnormal) is responsible for the difference between one unit of product and another, or between specifications and customer requirements. It is present in all processes. When present in one or more characteristics of a product or process, it causes poor quality and customer dissatisfaction. Products or processes should be expected to vary, because no two things are exactly alike. Differences result from design specifications, material requirements, methods, tools, systems, machines, and people. As shown in Table 6.1, variation can be interpreted as either (1) indicating good or bad performance, or (2) resulting from common or special causes. The variation that indicates good or bad performance forms the basis for inspection of products or services. It is the basis of accepting or rejecting a lot. One problem with this view of variation is that it does not provide any information on the causes of variation. Therefore, it does not provide enough useful information for improvement. The view of variation based on common and special causes provides a basis for action on the process.

Table 6.1: Interpretations of Variation

Types of variation	Integration elements			
	Focus elements	Objective	Rationale	Methods and tools
Variation that indicates good or bad performance	Process outcomes for products and services	Outcome classified as acceptable or unacceptable	The needs, desires, and wants of the customer	• Specifications • Performance indicators • Budgets • Goals • Forecasts
Variation that results from common or special causes	Causes of variation in the process	Actions taken on the process	What the process is actually delivering	Control charts • $\overline{X}$ chart • $\overline{U}$ chart • C chart • P chart • σ chart

Sources of Variation

Variation is a common phenomenon that should be expected to be present in all processes. Figure 6.1 lists sources of variation for manufacturing and administrative processes: material components, method and process components, environmental components, people components, machine components, and measurement/timing components. By understanding the sources of variation, it is possible to determine the shape of the distribution curve for parts produced by any process. Each of the sources of variation is discussed in the following sections.

Material Components

Material variations are primarily due to differences among part tolerances, changes in specifications, and type of material. Variations may also be due to specific components, subassemblies, and grades. For example, steel has different grades; aluminum has different specifications. The quality of products can easily be affected by the process material and the quality of supplier parts.

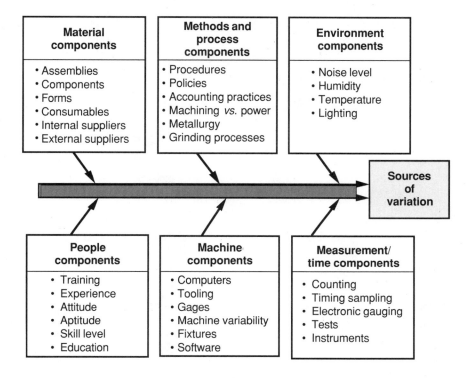

Figure 6.1: Typical Sources of Variation in Manufacturing and Administrative Processes

Method and Process Components

Method and process variation results from differences in interpretation and use of procedures, policies, practices, and process design specifications. A process can be defined as a set of causes and conditions that come together repeatedly to transform inputs into outcomes. The inputs might be people, materials, or information. The outcomes include products, services, behavior, or people. The variation seen when measuring pieces from a process is the result of two types of causes: (1) chance causes—those that cannot be prevented—which are continuously active and are built in as part of the process, and (2) assignable causes—those that can be prevented—which can be detected because they are not always active in the process. If variations in the product are primarily due to chance causes alone, the product will vary in a normal, predictable manner.

The product is said to be stable. As shown in Figure 6.2, assignable causes can distort the normal distribution curve. Process variation can be evaluated using statistical process control. A new process will cause variation through the learning curve and user unfamiliarity.

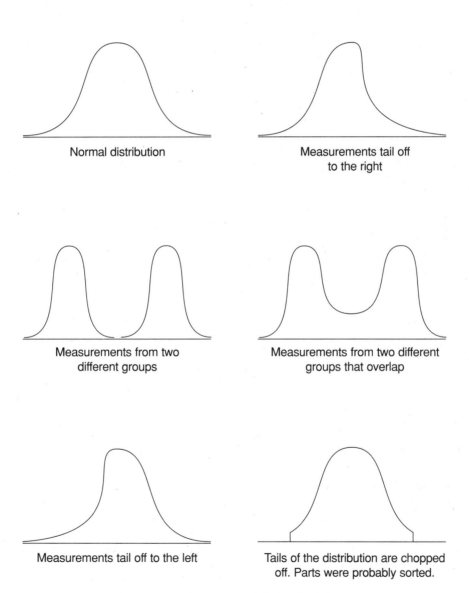

Normal distribution

Measurements tail off
to the right

Measurements from two
different groups

Measurements from two different
groups that overlap

Measurements tail off to the left

Tails of the distribution are chopped
off. Parts were probably sorted.

Figure 6.2: Distortions of the Normal Curve

Environmental Components

Environmental variation comes from regulations and specifications, usually external. Factors such as noise level, humidity, temperature, and lighting can affect quality performance and productivity. Some environmental factors such as humidity are not easily controlled due to their interrelationship with other factors such as temperature. The difficulty in handling environmental variation can also come from complexity and volume of work. The length and complexity of the work affects the error rate, performance, and effectiveness.

People Components

The ability to perform a task, intelligence, training, skill level, methods of learning, attitude, aptitude, and perceptions of quality and productivity all vary from person to person. Various individual attributes also vary over time for each individual.

Machine Components

Machine variation comes from differences in tolerances, specifications, and wear of equipment, tools, and machinery. Machine components also include items such as computers (hardware and software), material handling tools, and injection molding machines.

Measurements/Time Components

Variations due to measurements are from sources such as gauging, electronic instrument testing, counting, and sampling. Also, individuals and processes show variation over time in their performance, quality, and productivity. The performance of any person or process can vary significantly from one day to the next. Depending on the type of work, experience level, and skills, error rates of individuals can also vary with time.

Common and Special Causes of Variation

Variation in a quality characteristic has two types of causes: common causes and special causes.

Common Causes

Common causes are sources of chance variation that are always present because of small day-to-day variables. These causes are inherently part of the process (or system) and affect everyone working in the process. They are typically due to a large number of small random sources of variation. Common causes also contribute to the output variability because they themselves vary. Each common cause typically contributes a small portion to the total variation in process outputs. Common causes usually have a nonsystematic, random appearance. Process or system variability is defined in terms of common causes because they are regular contributors. The variables involved in common causes may change slightly from day to day, but this is natural. They will always be present, and the one way to stay ahead of this situation is to plan for it.

Special Causes

These are causes that do not occur naturally and are unusual. These types of causes are not part of the process (or system) all of the time or do not affect everyone but arise because of specific circumstances. Special causes are sporadic contributors and are due to some specific circumstances. Process or system variability is defined without them. These causes contribute to output variability because they vary.

Measures of Variation

To understand the magnitude of variation, it is important to measure performance of a process. The pattern of variation may not always tell the whole story about process output, because to look at the process output, part of the material must be measured. Measuring something is itself a process, so there is also variation in the measurement system just as there is variation in material or machine. To determine the true cause of variation in the process, the variation in the measurement system must be separated. The expression for separating the variation in the measurement system from the variation in the measured process output, to obtain the true variation in the process, is

Measured variation in process – Variation in measurement system
= True variation in process

Using this expression, it is easy to decide whether to work on the measurement system or the process or both. The key is to use the measure to improve performance by controlling sources of variation.

Two Measures of Variation

The two most commonly used measures of variation are the range and standard deviation. These measures enable users to understand the pattern of variation and actions that can be taken to remove the causes of variation.

Range

The range is the difference between the smallest and the largest value in a sample. It is expressed as

$$\text{Range } (R) = X_{i(\text{max})} - X_{i(\text{min})}$$

where

$$X_{i(\text{max})} = \text{largest value in the data set}$$
$$X_{i(\text{min})} = \text{smallest value in the data set}$$

To illustrate how range should be calculated, consider the data presented in Figure 6.3. The highest value (longest time) to complete a specific computer assembly task is 28 minutes and the lowest is 18 minutes. The range of times to complete the task is 28 minutes minus 18 minutes, which equals 10 minutes.

Standard Deviation

The standard deviation shows how much variation or spread there is in the sample data collected. It also describes how the data cluster around the most likely or average value for the sample. The standard is the square root of variance. The sample variance is used to estimate the population variance of the collection (data set). The higher the variance, the greater the spread of the data being analyzed. The standard deviation can be viewed as the tool that allows a sample to be used to predict the performance of an entire population. It is a better estimate of the variation than range. The expression for calculating standard deviation is

$$S = \sqrt{\frac{\Sigma (X_i - \bar{X})^2}{n - 1}}$$

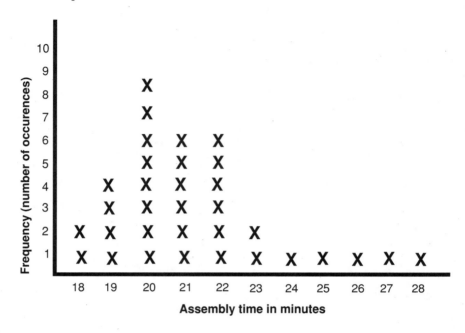

Figure 6.3: Histogram of Time to Complete Computer Assembly

where

S	=	standard deviation
X_i	=	individual measurement
$\bar{X}$	=	average of all measurements
n	=	sample size
$\sqrt{}$	=	square root
Σ	=	sum of

Standard deviation helps to determine the amount of variation in the sample data. It also helps analysts to see how data are grouped around the average or mean value. Whenever the variation is normal without any special causes, the following will be true.

- 99.7 percent of the data will be within 3 standard deviations above and below the mean.
- 95 percent of the data will be within 2 standard deviations above and below the mean.

- 68 percent of the data will be within 1 standard deviation above and below the mean.

Since 3 standard deviations cover almost 100 percent of the possible data, this measure is used to analyze processes. This is not possible when there are special causes.

Controlling Variation

How to Control Special Causes of Variation

Special causes present an opportunity for improvement in about 6 percent of cases encountered. To control special causes (1) change or fix the process, (2) use real-time data to obtain the right special causes signal, (3) implement early warning control indicators throughout the operation, (4) use the controls to search for assignable causes, and (5) continually seek avenues to change a higher level system to prevent special causes from reoccurring or, if the results are good, to retain the lesson. Special causes can be removed by operators or supervisors, although some special causes require intervention and action by management.

Common causes present an opportunity for improvement in the remaining 94 percent of typical situations. To control common causes, take the following actions: (1) Change the process, which may require training of employees, management, and staff. (2) Design an experiment to investigate cause-and-effect relations and use special improvement tools to correct common causes identified. (3) Improve measurement processes if measuring contributes significantly to the observed variation.

Other Strategies for Controlling Variation

Tampering

Tampering is an action taken on a stable process in response to variation within statistical control. Tampering is any adjustment made by a machine or an operator to a process. The adjustment is usually in response to variation due to common causes.

Design for Producibility

During the design phase, the product should be configured so that performance is shielded against variation. Design for producibility also requires focus on appropriate definition of tolerances on all product and process parameters; control parts proliferation; standardization of parts and processes used for a defined product set; and the application of statistical process control tools at the design and prototype phases.

Use of Quality Tools for Process Control

This strategy involves the use of quality management tools such as statistical process control, simulation, short cycle process management, part standardization, and participative management practices to continually track, control, and eliminate the root causes of variation resulting from machines, materials, tools, people, environment, and methods.

Supplier-Process Owner Partnership

The process owner and the supplier must continually work together to eliminate variation in parts and materials. This is done by (1) using statistical process control principles and techniques to qualify the supplier, (2) instituting a process control system at supplier and process owner workstations, (3) controlling the total number of suppliers through quality and productivity criteria, (4) providing appropriate product working drawings and design criteria for the supplier, and (5) providing adequate communication channels between suppliers and process owners to allow healthy discussions on potential problems and solution strategies.

Process Management and Control

Process management and control involves the use of knowledge of quantitative methods, common sense, and tools with employee involvement to achieve specified goals of continuously improving quality and productivity. As shown in Figure 6.4, the focus is on continuous product and process improvement. This strategy involves using quality management tools to continually isolate, control, and eliminate variation. Controlling variation through this approach requires cooperation from the entire organization. Continuous improvement efforts help detect and eliminate variation due to changes in requirements. In order for process management and control to yield positive results, management must take full responsibility.

The manager who owns the process to be improved should be in charge. The use of continuous improvement action teams is also recommended. The team focuses on ongoing identification and reduction of variation as well as assuring that all identified improvement projects are

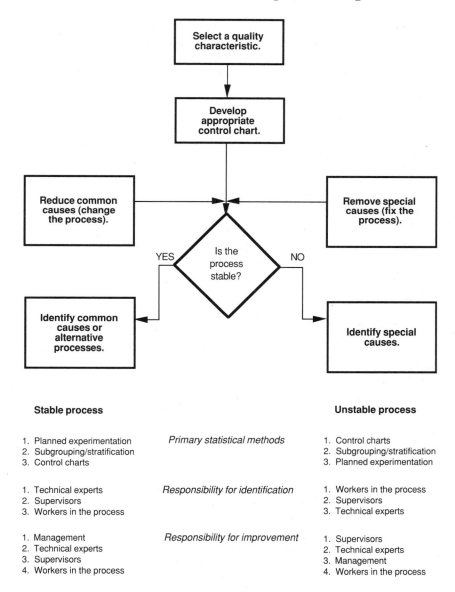

(*Source:* Nolan, T. W. and L. P. Provost. *Quality Progress*, August 1990, p. 77.)

**Figure 6.4: Methods and Responsibilities for Improvement
of Common and Special Causes of Variation**

implemented. To achieve maximum results the team must comprise both the suppliers (internal and external) and customers (self-unit, internal, and external). The team also works to certify processes by ensuring that the following requirements are met: operational requirements, output acceptability, process equipment, documentation, and specifications.

Summary

Variation in a production or service process is the number-one enemy of quality excellence. There is variation in all aspects of work processes. Misinterpretation of the concepts and patterns of variation can lead to significant quality and productivity losses. These losses can be minimized by understanding the assignable causes stemming from special and common causes and by implementing the right improvement actions. Both management and workers need to be trained in the use of basic statistical methods for identifying special and common causes of variation. Ongoing use of tools, techniques, and new technologies for process characterization and analysis is highly recommended in understanding assignable causes of variation. By eliminating variation during the design, within suppliers' processes, and within other external and internal processes, excellent product and process quality can be achieved. Variation is more than deviation from product and process specifications. It involves total and partial deviation from the ideal situation. The ideal situation is that which satisfies customer needs, wants, and requirements at minimum cost and with excellent quality.

CHAPTER 7

Process Management and Control

A customer- and market-driven enterprise must focus on ongoing process management and control with heavy use of statistics, data analysis, and interpretation to identify and correct quality problems at the source of production and service.

Control Charts

Control charts are statistical devices used to monitor the output of a process or system through the sample measurement of a specific characteristic and analysis of its performance over time. Control charts are used to study variations in a process that are attributed to special causes. Variation can be defined as the degree to which process output and yield are not identical. The primary goal in the use of control charts is to reduce fluctuation in a process until it is in a state of statistical process control.

Attribute Control Charts

Attribute control charts measure whether the product is defective, based on a number of quality characteristics. The attribute of interest can be based on a unit containing one or more defects or one source of failure to meet a specified requirement. The four types of attribute control charts commonly used are described in the following sections.

P *Chart (Fraction Defective Control Chart)*

The P chart is based on attribute data of the average number of defective units of product. It is used to control the overall defective fraction of a process. The P chart provides the proportion of defective product in a sample and is based on a binomial distribution. It is recommended when sample sizes are not equivalent. The data points, process average, and control limits are

Data points $\qquad P = \dfrac{\text{number of defective units}}{\text{number of units in sample}}$

Process average $\qquad \bar{P} = \dfrac{\text{total defective units}}{\text{total units observed}}$

Upper control limit $\quad \text{UCL} = \bar{P} + 3 \sqrt{\dfrac{\bar{P}(1-\bar{P})}{n}}$

Lower control limit $\quad \text{LCL} = \bar{P} - 3 \sqrt{\dfrac{\bar{P}(1-\bar{P})}{n}}$

$n = $ average sample size

NP *Chart*

The np chart measures the number of defectives in a sample of constant size. The data points, process average, and control limits are

Data points $\qquad np = \begin{array}{l}\text{number of defective units}\\ \text{in a subgroup}\end{array}$

Number of defective units in a lot of k subgroups $\qquad np = \dfrac{np_1 + np_2 + \ldots + np_k}{k}$

Upper control limit $\quad \text{UCL} = n\bar{p} + 3 \sqrt{n\bar{p}(1-\bar{P})}$

Lower control limit $\quad \text{LCL} = n\bar{p} - 3 \sqrt{n\bar{p}(1-\bar{P})}$

$n = $ subgroup sample size

C *Chart*

The C chart measures the number of defects in a sample when the opportunity in each area is equivalent for each sample. More than one defect may be recorded on a piece in the sample; the C value can be defined as the number of defects in a constant sample size. The data points, process average, and control limits are

Data points $\quad\quad\quad\quad\quad C = \quad$ number of defects

Process average $\quad\quad\quad \bar{C} = \dfrac{\text{total defectives}}{\text{number of samples}}$

Upper control limit $\quad$ UCL $= \bar{C} + 3 \sqrt{\bar{C}}$

Lower control limit $\quad$ LCL $= \bar{C} - 3 \sqrt{\bar{C}}$

U *Chart*

The U chart measures the average number of defects in a sample. It is applied when the number of units observed differs from sample to sample. The data points, process average, and control limits are

Data points $\quad\quad\quad\quad U = \begin{array}{l}\text{ratio of nonconformatives}\\ \text{to the sample size}\end{array}$

$$U = \dfrac{C = \text{ number of defects}}{n = \text{ sample size}}$$

Process average $\quad\quad\quad \bar{U} = \dfrac{\text{total number of defects } (C)}{\text{total process accepted } (n)}$

Upper control limit $\quad$ UCL $= \bar{U} + 3 \sqrt{\dfrac{\bar{U}}{n}}$

Lower control limit $\quad$ LCL $= \bar{U} - 3 \sqrt{\dfrac{\bar{U}}{n}}$

Variable Control Charts

Variable control charts measure the degree of a single variation of a single quality characteristic such as tolerance, weight, hardness, or temperature. These charts cannot be used with go or no/go data. They are helpful when detailed information on the process average and variations is needed for control of individual dimensions. The variable control chart uses an average of a small sample called a rational subgroup. The two most widely used variable control charts are the X and R charts. Data points, process averages, control limits, control chart factors, and distributions are presented in Tables 7.1, 7.2, and 7.3.

Sample Size for Attributes and Variable Control Charts

For X and R charts, the sample size recommended is usually four or five; for the percent defective chart P, samples of 25, 50 or 100 are recommended for inspection of results. For the C chart, a sample size of one is recommended.

Table 7.1: Definitions and Formulae for Variable Control Charts

Let
X	=	Individual observation
$\bar{X}$	=	Mean of a subgroup
R	=	Range of a subgroup
$\bar{\bar{X}}$	=	Grand means
$\bar{R}$	=	Average subgroup range
N	=	Number of observations in a subgroup
n	=	Number of subgroups

Mean: sum of observations divided by the number of observations
Range: difference between the largest and smallest number in the total observations
Subgroup: homogeneous small sample unit
Observations: value of a characteristic for individual unit

Chart	Data points	Average line	Upper control limit (UCL)	Lower control limit (LCL)
X	X	$\bar{\bar{X}} = \dfrac{\Sigma X_i}{N}$	$\bar{\bar{X}} + \dfrac{\Sigma 3\bar{R}}{d_2}$	$\bar{\bar{X}} - \dfrac{\Sigma 3\bar{R}}{d_2}$
$\bar{X}$	$\dfrac{\Sigma X_i}{N}$	$\bar{\bar{X}} = \dfrac{\Sigma X_i}{n}$	$\bar{\bar{X}} + A_2\bar{R}$	$\bar{\bar{X}} - A_2\bar{R}$
R	X maximum $- X$ minimum	$\bar{R} = \dfrac{\Sigma \bar{R}_i}{n}$	$D_3\bar{R}$	$D_3\bar{R}$

Table 7.2: Factors for Variable Control Charts (*X* and *R* Charts)

Sample Size (*n*)	Average (*A₂*)	Range D3	Range D4	Standard Deviation (*d₂*)
2	1.880	–	3.268	1.126
3	1.023	–	2.574	1.693
4	0.729	–	2.282	2.059
5	0.577	–	2.115	2.326
6	0.483	–	2.004	2.534
7	0.419	0.076	1.924	2.704
8	0.373	0.136	1.864	2.847
9	0.337	0.184	1.816	2.970
10	0.308	0.223	1.777	3.078
11	0.285	0.256	1.744	3.173
12	0.266	0.284	1.717	3.258
13	0.249	0.308	1.692	3.336
14	0.235	0.329	1.671	3.407
15	0.233	0.348	1.852	3.472

Table 7.3: Attribute and Variable Control Charts

Chart	Name	Type of data	Distribution
P	Fraction defective	Attribute	Binomial
np	Number defective	Attribute	Binomial
C	Number of defects	Attribute	Poisson
U	Defects per unit	Attribute	Poisson
X	Individual measurement	Variable	Normal
X̄	Averages	Variable	Normal
R	Ranges	Variable	Normal

Control Chart Construction

The following steps are recommended for constructing control charts.

Step one: Understand the process from which variation in process output is to be monitored.

Step two: Select the variables to be controlled and charted.

Step three: Determine the size and methods of obtaining subgroups from the process output.

Step four: Choose the type of control chart to be used (*P, np, R, C, X, x,* or *U*).

Step five: Collect data and plot until the period is considered representative of the normal operation of the process (30 or more points are desirable).

Step six: Connect the data points for readability.

Step seven: Calculate the center line of the chart—that is, the average sample.

Step eight: Calculate the upper and lower control limits and set the trial control limits.

Step nine: Review the control limits based on the age of the data (usually 25 points or more) and the state of the process.

Interpretation of Control Charts

Control charts can be useful for detecting assignable causes responsible for process variation if they are appropriately interpreted and used. The key indicators for reviewing control charts are process points; process averages; upper and lower control limits; variation in process points, trends, or patterns; and root causes (assignable) for problems. Typical variations in process points include runs, successive points on one side or either side of the process averages, and cycles, a unique pattern of causes. Key actions implemented to address process problems must also be identified and tracked, and projected improvement must be based on implemented actions with a benefit date.

As shown in Figure 7.1, in evaluating the process runs, the control chart is directed into zones. Each zone is one standard deviation wide. Between the upper and lower control limit are six standard deviations. The centerline divides the control into two zones of three standard deviations each. Tests for instability using control charts of process are determined by the following:

1. A single point falls out three standard deviations beyond zone A.

2. Two of three successive points fall in zone A or beyond the odd point.

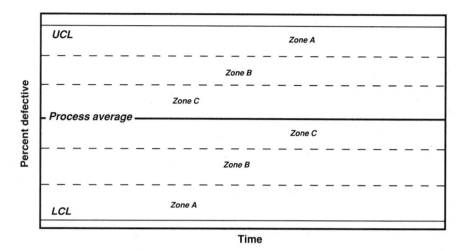

Figure 7.1: Control Chart Zones for Applying Tests for Instability

3. Four of five successive points are in zone B or beyond.

4. Eight successive points fall in zone C or beyond.

5. One or more points are outside the upper and lower control limits on the charts.

6. A run of seven or more points is above or below the process average centerline.

7. Cycle or nonrandom patterns of the data points are seen on the charts.

8. Eight successive points are on the same side.

9. Any 11 or 12 successive points are on the same side.

10. Any 13 or 15 successive points are on the same side.

Definition of Assignable Causes

Assignable causes responsible for variation in a process average performance may be monitored by points attributed to special causes, such as differences among machines, differences among operators, operator skill level, differences in product, influence of external factor, interrelationship among process variables, introduction of new product, instability in performance rates, and imbalance in process parameters.

Environmental Constraint Causes

These are factors which influence the process performance but cannot be directly altered by changes within the process. Examples are regulations and specifications.

Continuation Causes

Continuation causes are responsible for variations in the process which cause ongoing problems in particular aspects of the process. These types of causes are best solved by understanding the interrelationships among process parameters.

Maintainable Causes

Maintainable causes are responsible for variations in the process that cause monitored points to be maintained at a given level.

Sporadic Causes

Sporadic causes are responsible for large variations in the process performance monitored by points that exhibit random occurrences. The process and equipment characterization methods help to determine the effect of fixture, adjustment of tools, and equipment impact on the final output. Process characterization provides a unique approach for detecting possible assignable causes before they develop. It usually reveals frequency of occurrence for machine and tool-related defects, and frequency of defect occurrence due to adjustments.

Understanding Process Patterns of Variation

Emphasis should be placed on understanding the pattern of variation and pinpointing assignable causes of the variation. Within the process of any system operated over a period of time, typical patterns develop. It is important for the process control analyst to recognize these patterns for better interpretation and analysis of process problems root causes. The 14 most common patterns are presented in Figure 7.2 and discussed in the following sections.

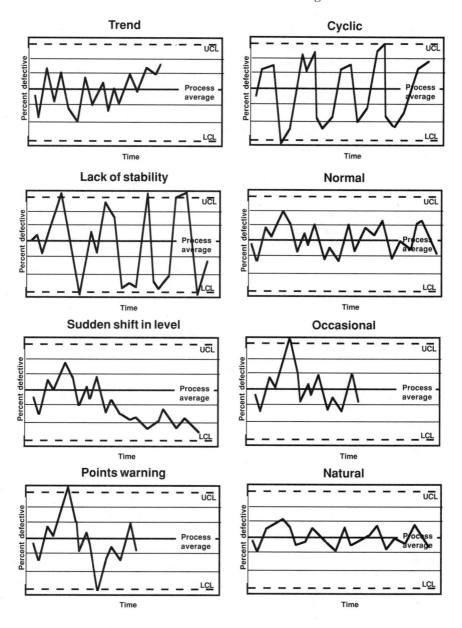

Figure 7.2: Common Patterns in Control Chart Analysis

(continued on next page)

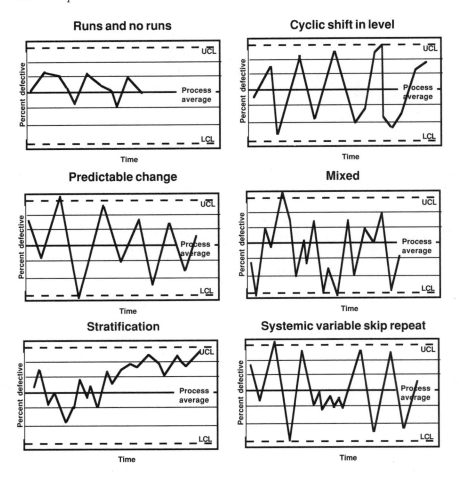

Figure 7.2 *(continued)*

Trend

A cumulative trend, usually consisting of seven or more consecutive points, indicates that the process is drifting. The pattern may be a gradual rise or fall to either portion of the control chart. The possible cause of the trend may be tool wear, deletion of reagent, or a decline in human efficiency owing to fatigue.

Lack of Stability

This pattern reflects a high level of large fluctuations within the process. Possible causes of the fluctuations may be overadjustment of process parameters such as material, tools, and equipment, and overcontrol of the process.

Sudden Shift in Level

A stable process will experience a sudden shift in level when new equipment, a new operator, or new materials are introduced to the process. A difference in product mix and configuration may also shift the process level.

Points Warning

When points are outside the upper or lower control limit, a special assignable cause is often responsible; for example, a high level of machine misinsertion within a given time period or a lack of operator training for a given task.

Cyclic

Differences among work shifts, operators, temperature, and other factors may result in a consistent pattern of repeated low and high points that occurs periodically almost within the same time intervals.

Normal

A normal pattern occurs within the control limits. It is usually based on random variation.

Occasional

These are points that occur outside the control limits with no consistent pattern. Such "freaks" are usually caused by the interaction of multiple factors, which is difficult to analyze. The best source for pinpointing causes is in the design of the experiment.

Natural

The process is fairly stable with no significant variation. The state of control is maintained consistently over time.

Runs and No Runs

This pattern indicates too many points or too few points on one side of a control chart centerline. This pattern could be caused by using the wrong specification for production, such as wrong equipment parts.

Predictable Change

This pattern shows a point-to-point variation that is easily identified. The variation is usually caused by similar or same cause, such as the level of tool wear.

Stratification

These are unnaturally small fluctuations that often appear around the centerline of the control charts.

Mixed

A few points near the centerline of the control chart show a seesaw effect. This pattern is usually caused by differences among sources of material and types, difference in training levels between operators, multiple machines, multiple tools, and different temperatures.

Cyclic Shift in Level

This pattern occurs when items such as a new material are introduced to the process at the same time internally or seasonally. A seasonal variation in humidity and temperature levels that affects tools and equipment within the process can also cause this pattern.

Systematic Variable Skip Repeat

This pattern is characterized by a predictable point-to-point variation that occurs within a given time interval. The predictable point-to-point variation often follows a different steady-state level in subsequent time periods.

Process Improvement Through Error Prevention

Production and service processes must be analyzed, reviewed, and improved on an ongoing basis. The goal should be to make the process simpler, the job easier, and the product more nearly perfect. Figure 7.3 depicts the quality improvement cycle and the overall defect correction process. Individuals and work teams should be encouraged to adopt a new error-prevention philosophy that focuses on quality at the source and total customer satisfaction. Emphasis on error prevention should be thorough, developing organized and systematic methods for performing work, ongoing identification of quality error sources, quality error

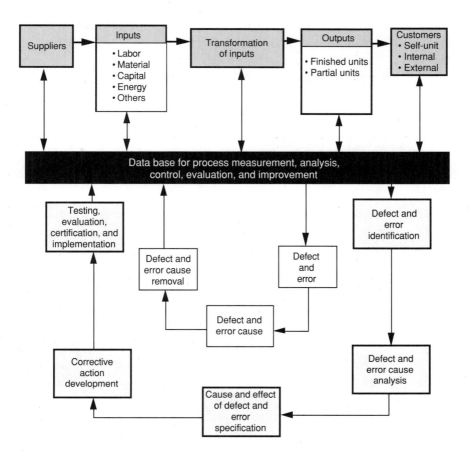

Figure 7.3: Quality Improvement Cycle

analysis, identification of quality error correction remedy, and implementation of quality error removal remedies.

The following steps are recommended for performing, process analysis, control, and improvement.

Step one: Understand the current process and task boundaries for the customer, organization, and supplier. Perform a thorough analysis of all production and service variables such as people, equipment, and materials.

Step two: Create a realistic awareness of the improved process. Convince others that a breakthrough is needed and that improvement is possible and desirable.

Step three: Specify opportunities for improvement by key process parameters and identify the important projects. Focus on problems that are most important. Production and service processes cannot be improved at random; it is important to identify specific projects for quality improvement. The entire work force should be encouraged and motivated to constantly review work processes for improvement. Improvement occurs through dedicated team effort that focuses on carefully selected projects.

Step four: Specify the scope of the improvement effort by process and task levels. Define responsibility for results.

Step five: Organize for breakthrough in knowledge and specify how to obtain required data.

Step six: Pilot the proposed improvement in the process. Focus on a few of the most important vital projects. Conduct process improvement analysis. Collect and analyze data required and recommend specific process improvement actions needed.

Step seven: Implement the recommended improvement, techniques, tools, and methods. Institutionalize the new ideas in the process. Evaluate and verify that the proposed improvement has occurred. Obtain feedback from both management and employees on the proposed improvement.

Step eight: Ensure that action plans are in place to control resource utilization. Monitor results from the new mix of resources to ensure that desired results are obtained. Determine the effect of proposed changes on people, processes, and the organization. Develop strategies to overcome resistance to change. Follow up periodically and repeat all steps for new opportunities. Implement adequate controls to hold the new level of improvement in productivity, quality, and total customer satisfaction.

Definition and Description of Sigma and a Normal Distribution Curve

Sigma is a statistical measure of the quality confidence of a product or process. When the number of sigma units is small, say one, product quality is not very good. The number of defects per million opportunities for a defect would be intolerable. When the number of sigma is large, say seven, quality would be excellent. The number of defects per million opportunities would be extremely small. For example, a product produced at six sigma exhibits no more than 3.4 defects per million opportunities at the part and process levels. As shown in Figure 7.4, the sigma approach to quality improvement requires clear definition of product and process requirements, understanding of tolerances required for each and every product, adequate measurement of process capability, and ongoing focus on improving product and process characteristics, including all input factors that drive the processes. Attaining six or seven sigma product quality will provide the following benefits.

- Achieve total customer satisfaction through virtually zero defective products.

- Reduce costs involving scrap, rework, and parts recycling.

- Increase market share through new business and current satisfied customers.

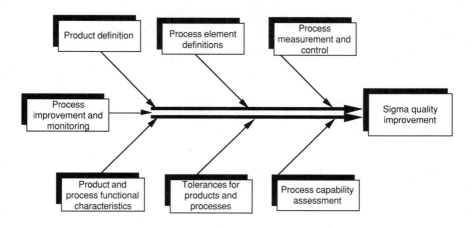

Figure 7.4: The Sigma Approach to Quality Improvement

• Reduce product delivery times through reduction in design and manufacturing cycle time.

When plotted on a frequency distribution chart, the normal curve is bell-shaped, as shown in Figure 7.5. With a normal curve, 99.99 percent of the data fall within plus or minus six standard deviations of the mean; 95.4 percent of the data fall within plus or minus one standard deviation of the mean. Most control charts have control limits that are also plus or minus three standard deviations from the mean. This means that random data from a constant, perfectly centered normal population will fall

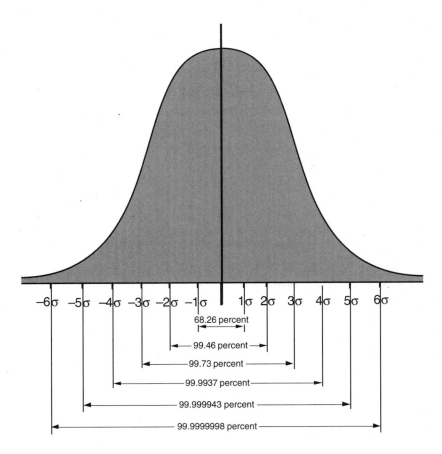

Figure 7.5: Typical Areas Under the Normal Curve

within the control limits 99.7 percent of the time. Since the probability of a random sample falling outside the control limits is so small, investigation usually shows that data outside the limits do not belong to the same population as the rest of the data. A normal curve such as the one shown in Figure 7.5 requires a very large number of intervals (or classes) that are extremely small as well as extensive data.

Applying the Six-Sigma Concept

When a product is at six sigma, the quality of the product is high. The probability of producing a defect is extremely low. To apply the six-sigma concept, use the following steps.

Step one: Identify the products and services by operational work units.

Step two: Identify key customers for the products and services using historical or current data on sales revenue and profit.

Step three: Identify business needs, wants, and requirements, and communicate them to suppliers, process owners, and internal customers.

Step four: Define process steps for performing work. Identify those that add value to the products and services and eliminate those that do not.

Step five: Determine outputs for each operational work unit and units for measurement.

Step six: Determine how many opportunities there are for a nonconformity or defect to occur in a particular product or service.

Step seven: Count the actual number of defects associated with that product or service. Use this information to determine how many defects per million.

The computation steps are as follows:

Step one: Count mistakes or defects associated with the product or service.

Step two: Calculate defects per unit (DPU) for each unit produced.

Step three: Multiply DPU by 1,000,000 and plot versus time. This is one version of the control chart.

Step four: Calculate defects per million opportunities for error to determine the sigma for the product or service.

Step five: Determine the average number of opportunities for error in one unit of product or service as perceived by the customer.

Step six: Multiply DPU by 1,000,000 and divide by the average number of opportunities for error.

$$\frac{\text{DPU} \times 1,000,000}{\substack{\text{Average opportunities} \\ \text{for error in one unit}}} = \text{Defects per million (DPM)}$$

Step seven: Plot DPM versus time to create the second version of the sigma control chart.

Step eight: Determine the approximate sigma level of product, service, or process using Table 7.4. The number of parts or process steps with the associated sigma level can be determined using Table 7.5. The rolled-throughput yield with the associated total defects per unit can be determined using Table 7.6.

Implementing the Six-Sigma Concept

Harry of Motorola, Inc. (1987), presents a four-phase approach for achieving six-sigma capability.

Phase One

This phase, related to process definition, involves physically defining the limits of the process—where it begins and ends in relation to the total

Table 7.4: DPM with Associated Sigma Level

Number of defects per million opportunities for error	Associated sigma level
66,910	3.00
22,750	3.50
8,210	4.00
1,350	4.50
235	5.00
32	5.50
3.4	6.00

Table 7.5: An Overall Yield Versus Sigma Level (Distribution Shifted +1.5)

Number of parts (steps)	+3σ	+4σ	+5σ	+6σ
1	93.32%	99.379%	99.9767%	99.99966%
7	61.63	95.733	99.839	99.9976
10	50.08	93.96	99.763	99.9977
20	25.08	88.29	99.536	99.9932
40	6.29	77.94	99.074	99.9864
60	1.58	68.81	98.614	99.9796
80	0.40	60.75	98.156	99.9728
100	0.10	53.64	97.70	99.966
150		39.38	96.61	99.949
200		28.77	95.45	99.932
300		15.43	93.26	99.898
400		8.26	91.11	99.864
500		4.44	89.02	99.830
600		2.38	86.97	99.796
700		1.28	84.97	99.762
800		0.69	83.02	99.729
900		0.37	81.11	99.695
1000		0.20	79.24	99.661
1200		0.06	75.88	99.593
3000			50.15	98.985
17,000			1.91	94.384
38,000			0.01	87.880
70,000	Use for benchmarking			78.820
150,000				60.000

Table 7.6: Total Defects per Unit with Associated Rolled-Throughput Yield

Total defects per unit	Rolled-throughput yield (%)
5.3	0.3
4.6	1.0
3.9	2.0
3.5	3.0
3.2	4.0
3.0	5.0
2.3	10.0
1.9	15.0
1.6	20.0
1.4	25.0
1.2	30.0
1.0	35.0
0.9	40.0
0.8	45.0
0.7	50.0
0.6	55.0
0.51	60.0
0.43	65.0
0.36	70.0
0.29	75.0
0.22	80.0
0.16	85.0
0.10	90.0
0.05	95.0
0.00	100.0
Rolled-Throughput Yield (%) = $100\ e^{-d/u}$	

manufacturing flow. Figure 7.6 illustrates the nature of such a flow. Through process definition, the limits of the battlefield are defined, so to speak. Also, during this phase all of the key inspection and test parameters are identified. In addition, by means of brainstorming, all of the known independent parameters are established. In turn, these factors are

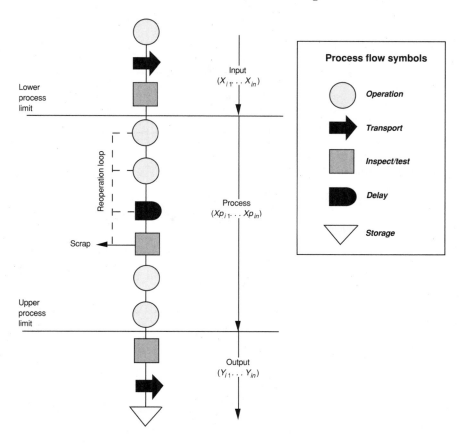

Figure 7.6: Sample Process Flow Diagram Showing Process Limits

placed in a cause-and-effect matrix to provide a process "scorecard" (see Figure 7.7). After all, when the action starts, you can't tell the players without a program.

Phase Two

Phase two establishes the capability of the process to attain a certain level of quality with respect to key product parameters. Such analyses are performed at two levels. A macro or global capability study is undertaken using discrete or attribute data. This establishes the overall process state of affairs. Expressing process performance in 6 units C_p creates a better understanding of the process characteristics. In addition, such

4	1	–	–	2
1	2	1	3	–
3	4	2	–	–
3	4	2	–	–
–	12	–	2	19

Cause:
process parameter
(causal variables)

Effect:
product parameters
(improvement opportunities)

Figure 7.7: Sample Cause-and-Effect Matrix

indices provide a means to benchmark the process under consideration against engineering decisions on future process design efforts. Should the macro capability study provide undesirable results, a micro analysis is undertaken. A micro analysis involves stratifying product quality data using Pareto diagrams to prioritize optimization efforts during phase three. Also, it is possible that at this point there may be a need to collect continuous data at the variable or "knob" level so that such things as parameter control efficiency can be assessed in relation to the six-sigma model. This step most often involves the use of histograms and statistical process control (SPC) for continuous variables.

Phase Three

Phase three is related to the optimization of characteristics identified during the micro capability study. The intent is to improve quality performance by reducing the influence of the underlying cause system. This is accomplished by deriving realistic operating tolerances for the "vital few" variables within the cause system. To do this, the engineer must first determine which variables, as related to the key process steps, are leverage in nature. In other words, the engineer must determine which factors are variation sensitive. Such identification is most often made with statistical graphs, brainstorming techniques, fractional factorial experiments, Taguchi-style arrays, and similar techniques. In short, the tools of SPC are applied to track down the sources of product and process variation. By discovering the vital few steps, variables, and relationships, the engineer ultimately is able to "work smarter, not harder" when undertaking the task of controlling the process according to the model.

Next, the low functional limit (LFL) and upper functional limit (UFL) must be defined for each of the vital few factors. Figure 7.8 displays the basic nature of the process associated with structuring the functional or realistic tolerance for an independent variable. Usually this is accomplished almost exclusively with statistically designed experiments such as full factorial and response surface matrices. The reason is simple: to adequately improve a process, existing nonlinear and interactive effects must be determined to know how best to prescribe settings for the critical process parameters. One must be able to take advantage of such things if improvement is to occur. This approach is inefficient and cost prohibitive and often not capable of revealing optimum conditions. The result of this step is a set of "prediction limits" for each of the vital few variables. In other words, the optimization experiments allow the required functional limits or realistic tolerances to be defined such that a product characteristic behaves as desired.

Following this step, the engineer must match the new performance capability related to the vital few factors to the six-sigma performance model. This step is most often achieved by comparing real-time performance data, normally displayed in the form of a histogram, to the experimentally defined realistic tolerance width. If the 34 range of a histogram only consumes 50 percent of the realistic tolerance, then the variable would be said to be capable of 6σ control. Given this condition, $C_p = 2.0$. If $C_{pk} \leq = 1.5$, then effort must be expended to adjust the parameter mean m back on target such that $C_{pk} \geq = 1.5$. If this is done, one would expect the parameter to exceed the UFL or LFL only 3.4 times, or fewer, out of every 1,000,000 manufacturing cycles, assuming a cause system that exhibits typical shifts and drifts.

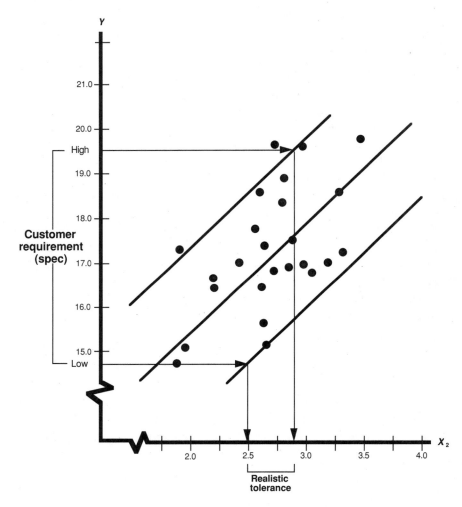

*Figure 7.8: Example of Functional or Realistic Tolerances
for an Independent Variable*

If the criteria for six-sigma capability is not met by this time, the engineer has three choices: (1) track down and eliminate the sources of variation if the parameter displays a great deal of nonrandom variation, assuming it would be economical to do so; (2) replace or otherwise modify the technology if the parameter does not meet the criteria but is free of assignable causes; or (3) alter the process to desensitize the critical variables, therein allowing the functional limits (UFL and LFL) of those variables to be redefined such that the six-sigma limits of the natural process distributions are compatible with their respective realistic tolerances. In this sense, the six-sigma manufacturing process would be achieved by: (1) desensitizing the leverage factors, (2) establishing garlands on factors which still exhibit a moderate form of leverage, and (3) opening the functional limits of the "trivial many" factors which are relatively noninfluential. In all instances, the concept of six-sigma tolerances would be applied. A manufacturing strategy along these lines is far more efficient and cost effective than simply "guard banding and automating everything in sight." Obviously, a fourth option would involve some combination of these alternatives.

Phase Four

Phase four is most closely tied to the classical uses of SPC-parameter monitoring and control. Once the vital few variables have been optimized, they must be controlled within their realistic tolerances. If this is not done, then the attribute control charts associated with the product performance characteristics will display unfavorable variation. In this sense, the charts will signal the alarm when a problem is about to surface.

Summary

Process management and control are key strategies for controlling variation in a production and service process to achieve ongoing measurement, improvement, and monitoring. The sigma approach to total quality improvement complements the error-prevention philosophy. This approach relies on the heavy use of statistics, data analysis, and interpretation to identify and correct quality problems at the source of production and service. Achieving six sigma in work processes requires effort and investment in ongoing training, process capability analysis, and improvement and long-term partnership between suppliers, process owners, and customers.

CHAPTER 8

Market-Driven Leaders, Teamwork, and Participative Management

Those who will lead the continuous improvement effort must be trained. Leadership vision is required to achieve excellence. All resources must be managed effectively and continuously. Achieving excellence in quality and productivity requires teamwork with suppliers, within enterprise work units, with customers, and between employees.

The Customer- and Market-Driven Leader

A customer- and market-driven leader (1) is committed to quality excellence, productivity improvement, total customer satisfaction, and employee well-being; (2) can inspire and communicate a vision for the enterprise; (3) shares power and information in a timely manner; (4) manages changes and conflicts; (5) knows when and how to use appropriate methods of decision making; and (6) serves as a role model to the work force.

A customer- and market-driven leader should possess qualities of transformational leadership. Transformational leaders commit themselves to a common enterprise and are resilient enough to absorb conflict, brave enough to be transformed by its accompanying energies, and capable of sustaining a vision that encompasses the whole organization.

The Customer- and Market-Driven Manager

A customer- and market-driven manager is responsible for (1) managing product and service requirements, (2) researching and responding to customer needs, wants, and desires, and (3) motivating and developing the work force to produce quality goods and services for internal and external customers. A customer- and market-driven manager should focus the mission and work product of the unit to satisfy the customer; be willing to listen to customer concerns and critiques; use customer suggestions as a base for continuous improvement in quality of product and service; continually train employees to treat customers as number one; make quality excellence a way of life for all employees; continuously track customer satisfaction and develop improved plans for products and services; develop business partnership with suppliers, process owners, and customers; and recognize that increasing market share, growth, and profitability come from quality, productivity, and total customer satisfaction.

Approaches for Improving the Quality of Market-Driven Management

The quality of management pertains to how well managers of operational units are able to plan, organize, integrate, control, delegate, measure, and direct. It also pertains to how well managers are able to (1) motivate people to do their best, (2) provide an excellent work environment and tools, (3) make timely decisions, (4) tolerate risks, (5) encourage innovation, and (6) reward accomplishment. Some of the most commonly used approaches for improving the quality of market-driven management are described in the next sections.

Quality Approach

This approach suggests that managers should evaluate and examine all facts carefully before making a business decision.

Personnel Approach

This technique suggests that a motivated, trained, and satisfied worker produces quality output without management intervention.

Cost Approach

This approach considers investments in labor, material, capital, energy, and technology as attempts to improve the quality of management by controlling cost and maximizing output.

People Approach

This approach focuses on identifying specific people- or product-oriented problems that affect employee performance. Specific techniques such as job enlargement or enrichment, training, job rotation, punishment, quality circles, management by objectives, employee promotions, and participative management address issues affecting employee performance. As shown in Figure 8.1, improving the quality of management

Figure 8.1: Elements in Improving Quality of Management

requires understanding the right organizational climate that stimulates the implementation of excellent management skills, tools, principles, and practice. Further, it instills responsibility and excellent managerial traits.

Developing Market-Driven Professionals and Managers

A four-stage career development process shown in Figure 8.2 is recommended for preparing market-driven professionals and managers. Each stage of the process is described in the following sections.

Stage one—assessment of market and business needs: The business environment is always changing. Management and employees must keep up with changes to stay competitive. The manager should periodically assess business needs and market requirements and the skills required to satisfy such needs.

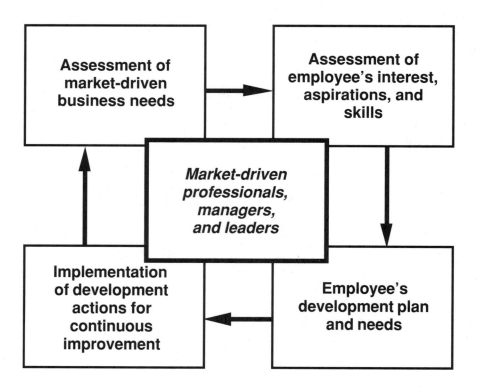

Figure 8.2: Market-Driven Professional Career Development Process

Stage two—employee's interests, aspirations, and skill assessment: Each employee should complete a professional-level resume. Through a career development planning session, employee and manager should together establish a realistic and achievable career goal. Manager and employee should be in general agreement concerning goals based on the employee's work history, present work, potential, and business opportunities. Short-range goals should cover the next two years; long-range goals should cover two to five years.

For example, the skills required two years ago to manage manual assembly of electronics components are quite different from those required for today's computer-integrated assembly method. Appropriate business needs and skills assessment should enable the manager to communicate and to prepare employees to meet business needs with ease.

Stage three—employee's development needs and plans: At this stage, the manager and employee search for appropriate development activities to help fulfill the goals and interests presented in stage two. Career development activities could be fulfilled by both formal education and on-the-job training programs. The manager documents the development plan with specific actions, dates, and responsibilities. A well-documented plan should be developed with the employee contributing his or her share. It is the manager's responsibility to provide the opportunities to try to meet the principles of the agreement.

Stage four—implementation of development actions and ongoing improvement: The roles and responsibilities in the market-driven professional development process are specified in Figure 8.3. A successful career development plan should accomplish at least one specific activity semiannually. The manager should have at least a semiannual career development meeting with the employee to make sure that development activities are accomplished. During this meeting, business needs and opportunities are discussed and the development plan revised as appropriate.

Participative Management and Teamwork

To achieve expected high-quality outputs and improved productivity, all units of the enterprise must work toward a common goal. Participative management plays a significant role in eliminating adversarial relationships within work units and encouraging the units to function in a cohesive manner.

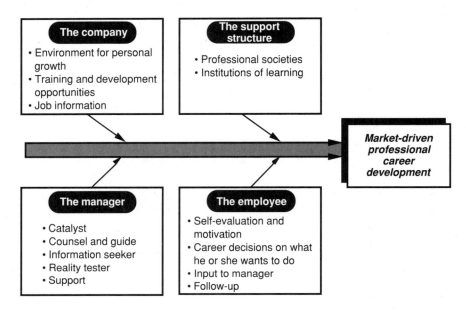

Figure 8.3: Roles and Responsibilities in Market-Driven Professional Career Development

Participative management can be defined as the extent to which management and employees work together on various functions required to produce products and services to satisfy the customer. The functions include decision making, problem solving, resource allocation, planning, training, improving performance, setting standards, goal setting, personnel problems, and general operations management.

The needs and wants of customers cannot be satisfied without teamwork, employee involvement and responsibility for work output, and good working relationships between management and employees. Participative management allows employees to take more interest in making meaningful contributions to work and to influence decisions that affect the final work output that goes to the customer. Participative management also increases the levels of commitment, productivity, innovation, and results at all levels of the enterprise. The participative process helps employee teams learn more about how an enterprise work unit functions and how they can make their areas work better.

Successful implementation of participative management requires that the development of team members' individual capabilities as one of the team's objectives. If management uses teams solely as a cost-reduction program or to manipulate employees for the organization's benefit, the program will fail. Management at all levels should support team efforts openly and unreservedly. Managers and supervisors should not feel threatened or take credit away from the team when improvements are made; involvement in team activities can enhance trust and cooperation between managers and team members. Membership on teams should be voluntary. If employees are forced to participate, they may believe that the process is just a management gimmick to make people work harder. Team spirit and group effort must be developed. Projects are not individual efforts. Team members should solve problems together and help each other learn and develop new skills. No criticism of people is allowed at any point in the process. The team must focus on the problems, not on personalities. Creativity and innovation should be encouraged. A nonthreatening, open atmosphere can be established and maintained in group meetings and management presentations. The leader must ensure that no members dominate the discussions or, conversely, feel limited in what they can express and contribute. Projects selected by the team members should relate directly to their work. The steering or advisory committee sets the general goals, objectives, and policies, and the teams choose the focus and procedures to meet these goals. Members become more responsible for their work when involved in making decisions regarding that work.

Management must endeavor to provide practical training in problem-solving techniques. It is essential that team members have the tools and skills needed for finding solutions and making recommendations on the projects they select. A problem-solving capability should be developed in employees, and an attitude of problem prevention must prevail throughout all team activities. Emphasis on quality and productivity excellence should be maintained at all levels.

Participative Management Skills

The focus elements of participative management shown in Figure 8.4 are discussed in the following sections.

Leading, Delegating, and Directing

This involves providing the vision for future improvement; encouraging the work force to participate in implementing new ideas; encouraging the

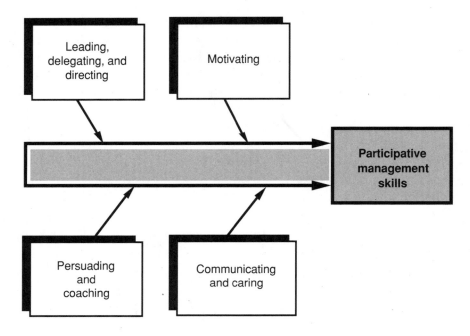

Figure 8.4: Participative Management Skills

team to take a leadership role in project management and to take risks to achieve challenging results; and directing the utilization of resources for effective solutions and results.

Motivating

The motivation of the work force should focus on job enlargement and enrichment, decision making, empowerment, recognition and reward, performance planning, and fostering a participative environment where innovation and creativity will flourish.

Persuading and Coaching

This involves the sincere effort of management to provide the right information and to communicate facts precisely about a given problem or subject; providing appropriate feedback; and demonstrating behaviors worthy of emulation.

Communicating

Management should focus on active listening to others' concerns and points of view, thereby establishing a healthy work climate and a good communication process. Focus should also be placed on highlights and main discussion points. A series of statements should be summarized into a comprehensive one. Encourage others to participate in discussions. Clarify opinions and points of view. Show empathy for other people's suggestions, feelings, and requests.

Caring

This involves providing support mechanisms and attitudes that make people feel good about being members of the team. It also requires working with people to improve poor performance. In correcting poor performance, managers should provide ongoing counseling and feedback on performance levels. Provide the required classroom and on-the-job training to correct deficiencies in skill level. Skills of the individual should be matched to the right job when necessary. Job rotation should be used to enhance skill level. The poorly performing individual must be given the chance to accept responsibility for gradual improvement steps to correct low performance level. Provide appropriate feedback, recognition, and reward for performance.

Elements of Fostering Teamwork

Good management maintains a balance between people and product management, as well as encouraging a participative approach to business management. Such a participative style allows for input to decision making, provides worker control over jobs, and encourages innovation, ownership of results, and accountability for actions.

There has to be an appropriately defined mission for individuals and the organization. The goals of the organization and of individuals must complement each other. Everyone within the organization must be aware of the common goals, and their role and required contributions to meet the objectives. The work environment should allow people to strive toward common objectives and results. Break down the barriers between management and functional areas. Recognize individual and group performance. Focus on adequate communication channels and information which enhance group knowledge and build trust among people. Vision seeks teamwork as a source of strength, not a threat.

Management should work on providing adequate balance between the desires and needs of individuals. Encourage teamwork along the line of a common goal which requires interdependence. Management attention is required on an ongoing basis to the people management issues that affect teamwork, cause friction, and affect productivity and quality improvement. The right management attention should provide an open-door policy that allows individuals and teams to discuss people and product management problems honestly in a nonthreatening manner, with the focus on respect for individual opinions, ideas, and values while achieving positive results for everyone.

Summary

Vision and strategies for quality excellence and total customer satisfaction can be created by participative leaders and managers. Implementation of specific ideas and programs that will lead to improvement requires the total support of the work force. The participative management process is recommended as a means for encouraging teamwork and for getting quality results through people. The responsibilities of customer- and market-driven leaders and managers involve (1) developing and supporting a customer-oriented quality policy and program, (2) implementing customer-based measures of performance throughout the organization, (3) supporting the lower-level workers in their quest for quality, (4) providing a work environment that fosters excellent quality performance, and (5) rewarding results in a timely manner. The key to success is empowering all people to give their best talent to provide the best products and services to the customer. Quality excellence and total customer satisfaction come from hard work, dedication, and commitment from customer- and market-driven leaders, managers, and employees.

CHAPTER 9

Implementing Continuous Improvement Projects and Overcoming Common Problems

Any quality or productivity improvement, no matter how small, is a change that affects people. People perceive change as a threat to their work habits, comfort, and security. The threat, in turn, creates emotional and psychological resistance.

Implementing Continuous Improvement Projects

The 9C principles shown in Figure 9.1—customer awareness, controls, coordination, cooperation, contribution analysis, communication, cost avoidance, commitment, and competence/congruence—are recommended for managing customer-driven quality and productivity improvement projects.

Principle One: Select Quality and Productivity Improvement Projects Based on Customer Awareness and Business Needs

Before embarking on quality and productivity improvement projects, it is important to understand the current business process and identify areas for improvement. Do a thorough analysis of all production and service variables. Use internal and external customer needs, wants, and requirements to create a realistic vision of the improved process. The quality improvement agent should help convince others that a breakthrough is needed and that quality improvement is possible and desirable.

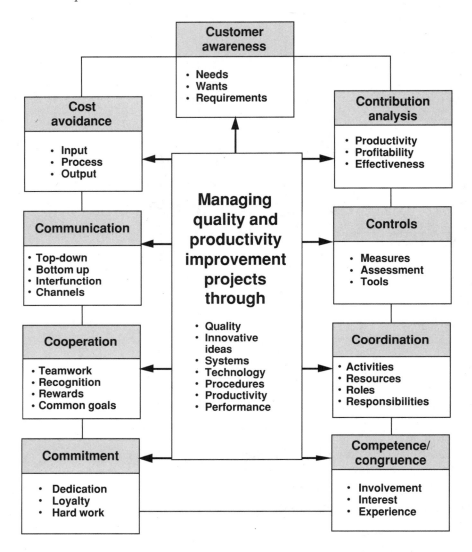

Figure 9.1: The 9C Principles for Managing Customer-Driven
Quality and Productivity Improvement Projects

Principle Two: Commitment—Obtain Employee and Management Commitment for the Quality and Productivity Improvement Project

The success of quality and productivity improvement projects depends on total commitment from both employees and managers. When everyone is committed to completing a project, it is usually successful. When everyone is psychologically involved in their work on a specific improvement project, higher levels of motivation, performance, and loyalty will result. Commitment from everyone also provides a strong base for resolving potential project problems and conflicts.

Principle Three: Create Competence and Congruence

Highly experienced professionals with technical and project management knowledge in quality and productivity should be selected as members of the team. These experienced professionals usually have contacts with external and internal experts in quality and productivity. Where such help is not available, the use of consultants and a task force is recommended.

Principle Four: Controls—Provide Controls to Monitor Customer-Driven Quality Improvement Projects

In managing quality issues and projects, it is important to define the objectives and understand the activities involved. Specific performance parameters such as cost curves and control charts should be used in measuring the results of implementing the objective. In addition, a schedule for the various activities has to be identified. Two techniques are recommended for controlling all the elements involved in a specific project.

Gantt Chart

A Gantt chart like the one shown in Figure 9.2 provides a means for arranging the list of activities to be accomplished. Activities are arranged vertically, while their schedules are displayed horizontally. The analyst monitors the completion of each task and tracks unfinished ones until completed.

Time (hours, days, weeks, months, and years)

Figure 9.2: A Typical Gantt Chart for a Productivity and
Quality Improvement Project

PERT Chart

The PERT (Project Evaluation and Review Technique) chart, as shown
in Figure 9.3, provides a means for managing the probability of success
for each task and highlights the earliest and latest times a given task can
be accomplished.

Principle Five: Coordination—Provide a Focal Point for
the Coordinating Quality Improvement Projects

Quality and productivity improvement ideas and activities need to be
coordinated. This can be achieved by designating a quality improvement
project manager to be in charge of all activities. The project manager,
working with other members of the project team, ensures that project
resources are controlled and allocated properly, and that the project is

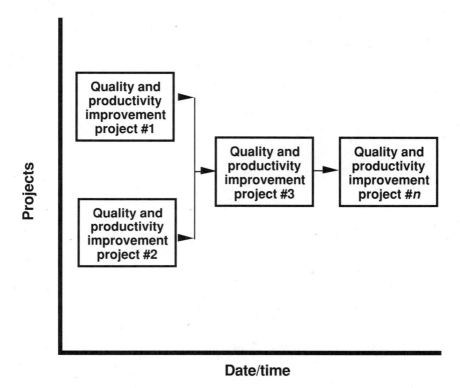

Figure 9.3: A Typical PERT Chart for a Productivity and Quality Improvement Project

going according to schedule. The project manager requires a good data base and tracking mechanisms for all activities. The successful project manager has good interpersonal skills, good organizational and planning abilities, and good judgment.

Principle Six: Communication—Provide Adequate Communication Channels

The status of productivity and quality improvement projects must be reviewed periodically by the people involved. Usually, the project manager ensures that regular meetings are held to discuss open issues that require resolution and also to obtain status on key accomplishments. Ongoing communication among project team members is required to keep things from falling through the cracks.

Principle Seven: Cost Avoidance—Provide Adequate Focus on Cost Avoidance

To avoid cost overruns in productivity and quality improvement projects, the project implementation phases cost posture should be monitored. Avoid additional features of functions without value added. At each phase of the project, careful attention must be paid to capital expenditure on fixtures, programming, human resources, and contract services. When vendors are responsible for project implementation, periodic cost postures must be requested and reviewed by the project leader.

Principle Eight: Contribution Analysis—Implement Measures to Monitor the Contribution of Each Phase of Productivity and Quality Improvement Projects

Each implementation phase of a quality and productivity improvement project should provide tangible results. For example, the machine characterization phase should enable the project leader to understand the pattern of performance of a given machine. The contribution analysis of each phase of the improvement project can be performed by using the variable and result mapping technique. This technique requires that for each activity or task performed, the expected result must be matched against the expected output and project goals and objectives. The next requirement is to pursue understanding of the causes of deviation from specifications. The variable mapping technique requires action to resolve project deviations promptly.

Principle Nine: Cooperation—Facilitate Cooperation Among Project Participants

Cooperation among members of the project implementation team is a key for success. If possible, the teamwork process should involve the designer, developer, implementers, and users of the new method or idea. Where the physical presence of representatives from all the functional areas is impossible, communication channels should facilitate information sharing to promote cooperation. The understanding of the goals and objectives behind the implementation of a new idea in the workplace by all members of the organization facilitates cooperation. Such understanding can be accomplished through project kickoff meetings at various levels of the organization.

Overcoming Resistance to Change

People will accept or resist change depending on how they are affected by it. By nature, people have some resistance to change because of fear of the unknown; they hope to avoid failure. Resistance to change—a desire to adhere to the familiar past—can be a major stumbling block in the manager's attempt to move the business forward. If people are confused or angry or do not agree with the change, the process becomes much more difficult.

One is likely to encounter the following five types of people when promoting and implementing change.

1. Those who perceive that they have no choice in change. It is happening regardless, and their role is to wait for the next turn.

2. Those who will do everything within their power to defeat the change, because it creates an extra burden on them. Such people always find several reasons why the change will not work. They try to convince the change agent to stay with the old method.

3. Those who do all the talking about how change is badly needed but take very little action.

4. Those who spend their energy wishing someone else or some new system will automatically do the work.

5. Those with keen interest in profitability through growth, continuous improvement, and effectiveness. Such people are the change owners, masters, agents, project champions, and leaders who get under the load, do the work, and design, promote, and implement the change required for success.

The strategy is to get all five categories of people convinced to a great extent. This can be done through emphasis on teamwork and effective communication. People must be informed about what the change will bring to their tasks and the organization's growth and profitability. It is often difficult to break away from an old pattern and accept a new one, but people are likely to accept a change when they fully understand the tangible and intangible benefits of changing from an old habit to a new one.

Preparing the Enterprise Team for Positive Response to Change

Figure 9.4 presents a model for effecting and managing change in a market-driven enterprise. Effective positive change to satisfy customer-driven

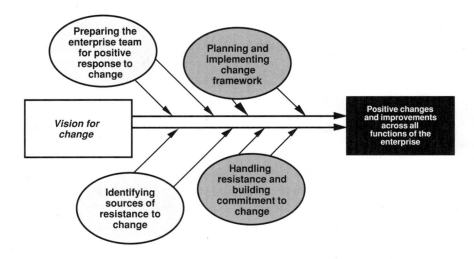

Figure 9.4: Continuous Change Management Model

needs requires preparing managers and nonmanagers to understand what is different in the competitive market environment and why innovative ways of running the enterprise business are required. The approach for preparing the enterprise team for change consists of the following steps.

Step one: Select leaders of the enterprise that are future oriented and inspired by change. Leadership vision, courage, empathy, humility, and wisdom are required to implement a change. The critical mass must be inspired and motivated to change. Generally, the work force will follow the leader's commitment to help mold change to the enterprise's and the customer's advantage.

Step two: Help business unit managers understand what is changing in the business environment and what change is all about. Managers must know that there is need to change.

Step three: Help managers understand how to define change and how to understand the management, communication, and training process involved in managing change.

Step four: Thoroughly understand the changes in business, both now and in the future. All changes should be planned and treated like a courtship.

Step five: Develop the managerial tools and skills required to manage change. These include analytical, behavioral, and organizational management skills, willingness to change, commitment to change, and the desire to manage change.

Step six: Recognize the informal organization and provide a positive climate to help those affected to respond and accept the change quickly. The enterprise can be viewed as a social system consisting of a loose network of small groups of people. People in these groups can form a strong bond of loyalty to each other. These groups should be used to institute change. If the informal groups and their leaders accept whatever change is being proposed, that change will occur smoothly. If they oppose the change, it may be nearly impossible to implement. Therefore, it is important to identify and get the informal groups involved in change execution and implementation.

Step seven: Develop change agents for change execution and effective implementation. It is very important for the leader of change to seek the active support of a critical mass of influential people. When such critical mass support is obtained, change execution and implementation occur smoothly.

Step eight: Assess the enterprise's readiness to make the change, allowing enough flexibility for people to prepare for the change and deal with consequences. Plans should be in place to deal with both the rational and irrational sides of change.

Planning and Implementing Change

The steps presented in Figure 9.5 are recommended to managers interested in introducing and implementing quality and productivity changes in their operational unit or organization.

Step one—diagnosis and business environment assessment: In diagnosing for change, employees should understand the business thoroughly and find out what is happening, what is likely to happen in the future, and how the anticipated changes will affect their organization. Specific attention should be paid to market-driven changes, customer expectations, technology changes, skill mix changes, product development cycles, regulations, competitors, cultural changes, and service and manufacturing capability.

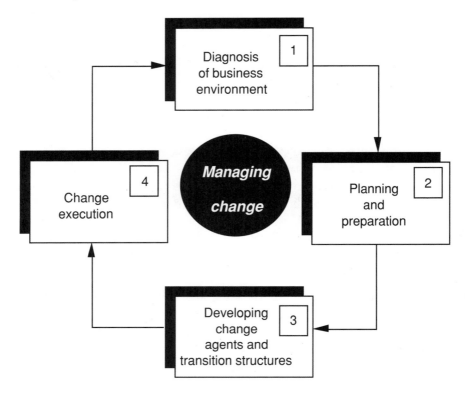

Figure 9.5: A Framework for Managing Change for Innovation and Productivity

Step two—planning and preparation: Most change effort begins with the identification of problems or through a need presented by a new market requirement. Change efforts involve attempts to reduce discrepancies between the real and the ideal. Reducing discrepancies between the actual and the ideal means thoroughly thinking through the change. In this step, participative management works very well. Planning and preparation include

- Describing the change and communicating anticipated benefits.
- Obtaining input from those who will be affected by the change and those who will help implement the change. Input from customers, employees, peers, superiors, and subordinates should be encouraged.

- Assessing the organizational readiness to make the change. This usually requires answers to the following questions.

  —What is the maturity level of the people involved?

  —Are they willing and able to make the change?

  —What leadership, decision-making, and problem-solving skills are available, and what are the assumptions behind the change?

  —What are the expected risks and benefits?

  —Is everyone ready to undertake the change?

- Preparing the change plan with various options and highlighting the preferred plan and timetable.

- Anticipating the skills and knowledge required to master and implement the change.

- Focusing on changes that are critical for success. Change most things only once, if possible, and encourage stability and routine in minor operations when appropriate.

Step three—develop change agent and transition structures: Change agents must have the skills to diagnose a situation and develop acceptable solutions. The roles of change agents include, but are not limited to, the following: facilitator, listener, participative designer, team leader, and catalyst. They must have the wisdom to know when to push the change versus when to lay back and let people accept the change with time. Humility can easily facilitate the implementation of change.

Successful change management cannot be achieved without the right communication channels. Appropriate new communication channels are required to get people involved and let them know why the change makes sense. When appropriate, create a transition team to oversee the change and develop policies and procedures that make implementation of the change easy.

Step four—change execution and implementation: Most change fails to yield expected results not because it is not good but because the mechanisms for implementation were not carried out properly. The following guidelines are recommended when implementing change.

- Understand the organization's climate and culture. Obtain the total support of everyone affected by the change. Have a good reason to make a change.

- Outline specific implementation steps for the change. Ensure that timing and content are realistic and open to new opportunity.

- Plan implementation activities ahead of time. Give people a chance to step back and take a look at what is going on. Use transition management teams as required.

- Provide appropriate training in new skills and coaching in new values required to implement the change.

- Encourage self-management. Let people know where they stand, and inform them of their responsibilities.

- Put a respected change master in charge of the process.

- Allow for withdrawal and return of people who resist temporarily. Encourage their participation and consider their input to make modifications in the change process as appropriate.

- Establish a clear review process for concerns and grievances that may arise. Prepare to help those who have special difficulty adjusting to the change.

- Use opportunity created by the change to reward. Create incentives for special efforts. Ask for input from knowledge groups and individuals who have helped to make things happen.

- Be flexible and willing to sacrifice time and resources to make the change happen. Do not expect too great a result overnight. Gradually seek improvements from the change.

- Find out who has implemented such change before and learn from their experience.

- Encourage a positive team attitude and strong enthusiasm to succeed. Use participative management to build a climate that fosters cooperation and involvement of the entire organization.

- Help people to get what they need and avoid what they do not need. Provide empathy and information to make people feel comfortable with the change.

- Use outside help when appropriate, and establish symbols of change through ongoing communication.

Implementing Change in Familiar Steps

The change implementation matrix presented in Figure 9.6 depicts a typical response by the work force to a proposed change. To implement a change successfully at any level of the enterprise, use the following steps.

1. Assess the magnitude of the proposed change and the vision for it.

2. Divide the change into manageable and familiar steps and specify implementation timing.

3. Communicate the change effectively.

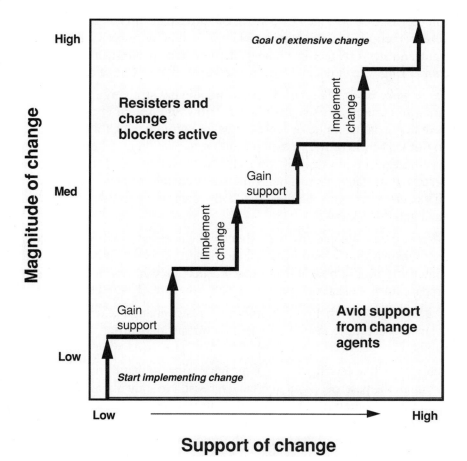

Figure 9.6: Change Implementation Matrix

4. Assess the potential response to the change. Identify potential avid supporters, undecided, workers, and resisters.

5. Develop and implement strategies to win the support of everyone, including the undecided and resisters.

6. Develop and implement actions to assist those affected by the change, and follow up on open issues.

Identifying Sources of Resistance to Change

Kanter (1985) identifies the following reasons why people resist change.

Loss of control: The way people greet a change has much to do with whether or not they feel in control of it. Change is exciting when it is done *by* people, but threatening when it is done *to* people. Most people want and need to feel in control of the events around them. Change could bring with it uncertainty and create a sense of loss of control.

Excess uncertainty: A second reason people resist change is when too much uncertainty exists. Simply not knowing enough about what the next step is going to be or feel like makes comfort impossible. If people do not know where the next step is going to take them, whether it is the organizational equivalent of "off a cliff" or "under a train," the change is perceived as dangerous. Then they resist change because they reason, "It's safer to stay with the devil you know than to commit yourself to the devil you don't know."

Surprise factor: People are easily shocked by decisions or requests sprung on them without groundwork or preparation. Their first response to something totally new and unexpected that they have not had time to prepare for is resistance.

The difference effect: People sometimes resist change when it requires them to become conscious of and to question familiar routines and habits.

Loss of face: If accepting a change means admitting that things were done wrong in the past, people are certain to resist. Nobody likes losing face in front peers. Sometimes making a commitment to a new procedure, product, or program carries with it the implicit assumption that the old ways are bad. This puts individuals in the uncomfortable position of either looking stupid for past actions or being forced to defend them—and thereby arguing against any change.

Concerns about future competence: Sometimes people resist change because of personal concerns about their future ability to be effective. They question if they can do it. They wonder how they can change and under what conditions. They also question whether they can operate in a new way. These concerns may not be expressed out loud, but they can result in finding many reasons why change should be avoided.

Ripple effects: People may resist change for reasons connected to their own activities. Change sometimes disrupts other plans or projects, including personal and family activities that have nothing to do with the job, and anticipation of those disruptions causes resistance to change.

More work: One reasonable source of resistance to change is that change requires more energy, time, and mental preoccupation than maintaining the status quo.

Past resentments: Another reason people resist change is negative experiences. It is the reality of organizational life that those cobwebs get in the way of the future. Anyone who has ever had a gripe against the organization is likely to resist when the organization tells them they now have to do something new.

Sometimes the threat is real: The last reason that people resist change is when the change poses a real threat. In many ways, this is the most reasonable of all causes. Sometimes a change does create a threat, even for winners. Change provides a tremendous opportunity, but even in that opportunity, there is some small loss. It can be a loss of the past, a loss of routines, comforts, and traditions, or maybe a loss of relationships that have become very close over time. Things will not, in fact, be the same anymore.

Change Implementation Checklist

Implementing change successfully requires understanding the total impact of change on the organizational's structure, people, business policies, procedures, and overall effectiveness. Successful implementation also requires anticipating potential adverse consequences of change. The master change agent seeks answers to the following questions.

1. What has to change in the business environment?
2. What is the magnitude of the change required for success?
3. What are some dimensions of the proposed changes?

4. How will the change affect the organization, employees, management system, quality of working life, and profitability?

5. Who is trained to manage the change?

6. What communication channel will be used for the change?

7. How will everyone be made part of the change?

8. What mechanisms and avenues are in place to handle grievances, resistance to change, and dislocations?

9. Is the management team equipped to deal with the physical, emotional, and intellectual aspects of change?

10. What is the timetable for making the change?

11. What are the anticipated short- and long-term impacts of the change on the enterprise?

12. What new skills, knowledge, and attitudes are required to make this change?

13. What incentives are in place to facilitate the change?

14. What potential risks and exposures are associated with the change, and what alternatives are in place to counter such risks and exposures?

15. Will the proposed change provide any disincentives for employees? Customers? Other organizations?

16. What benefits are most likely to be achieved by making the change?

17. What are the strengths and weaknesses of the individual/group undertaking this change?

18. What internal and external obstacles are likely to affect the implementation of the change?

19. What are the measures for success?

20. Is the change going to create a win/win situation for everyone?

Unwillingness to Change a Work Habit

After learning a pattern to perform a specific task, the pattern becomes a habit. It is often difficult to break away from the old habit and accept a new one. People must be educated about what productivity and quality improvement will bring to their tasks, and in addition must be shown the tangible and intangible benefits of changing from an old habit to a new one. A good strategy is to get everyone involved in all phases of the projects when possible.

Lack of Proper Planning

A productivity and quality improvement program can easily be unsuccessful if the requirements for start-up, key people, and total implementation of activities are not planned properly. It is important that appropriately trained people with knowledge of productivity and quality be made coordinators of improvement projects. Such coordinators must specify in great detail the key activities needed for improvement projects, who is responsible for them, when they will be completed, and the expected benefit date.

Fear of the Unknown

New productivity and quality improvement ideas may have some uncertainty because of unproven results. Most people are likely to be afraid of failure and as a result, they may resist the implementation of new concepts. All levels of management and employees must be educated about the importance of willingness to risk failure. If one new ideal fails, it does not prevent another good one from succeeding.

Lack of Appropriate Data Base

A productivity and quality improvement program should be based on an adequate data base with correct historical information. It is very important to involve all levels of management and employees during improvement program start-ups to ensure that adequate data and a description of procedures are provided.

Resentment of Criticism

Most people believe that they perform their tasks in the most effective and efficient manner and will resent criticism that proves otherwise. Criticism from productivity analysts, coordinators, and consultants should be constructive to avoid backlash. On the other hand, those receiving ideas must be willing to do away with a defensive attitude.

Everyone involved in the productivity and quality improvement program must have an open mind and the willingness to accommodate several different viewpoints.

Inadequate Sharing of Productivity and Quality Improvement Ideas

Productivity and quality gains obtained from improvement program must be distributed fairly to encourage continued innovation for additional ideas. Most organizations have formal suggestion programs, cost effectiveness programs, bonus programs, and awards programs specifically designed to reward contributions to productivity and quality improvement. Money is not the only source of motivation. Peer and superior recognition, promotions, additional challenges, job content, and others are also key sources of motivation.

Conflicting Compromise of Objectives

Productivity and quality improvement go together. Managers and employees must stay away from the notion that if productivity improves, quality will suffer. The tendency to push schedules when they are needed and push quality when it is wanted should be eliminated. Programs selected for improvements must satisfy dual objectives. People must be trained in how to manage conflicting objectives.

Complacency Resulting from Current Status

There is a tendency for an organization that is a leader in its industrial sector to feel so satisfied with its performance that it ignores ongoing assessment of its method of operation and recommendations for changes. Everyone within the organization must be trained to recognize that there is no limit to success through improvement. The more improvement ideas are implemented, the better off the organization will be financially.

Starting Off Too Big

Productivity and quality improvement issues can get complicated. The problems of the entire organization cannot be resolved overnight. For improvement programs to be successful, they must be started with reasonable projects that available resources can handle. Once the results and benefits of such projects have been obtained, bigger ventures can be attempted.

Summary

Managing quality and productivity improvement projects requires teamwork. Keeping people committed to improvement projects involves showing them the benefits to be derived. When people understand the benefits for the company and what they have to gain for their efforts, they tend to stay on the project team. The success of a quality and productivity improvement program depends upon people's capabilities and attitudes and how effectively changes are implemented.

CHAPTER 10

Conclusions

The quest to become a customer- and market-driven enterprise requires more than speeches and good intentions. Execution of well-defined continuous improvement strategies for quality, productivity, and total customer satisfaction is required.

Successful customer- and market-driven enterprises set goals, meet goals, raise the goals, and meet these new goals. They invest significant amounts of time and money on education and training. Customer- and market-driven enterprises use continuous improvement in quality and productivity to become world-class leaders. They stress total customer satisfaction rather than short-term financial performance. Managers and nonmanagers at all levels should be measured in terms of value and excellence. Emphasis should be placed on cross-functional team building and employee involvement. Employees across the enterprise should be given authority to make changes in work processes to improve quality and productivity. Success is built on continuous focus and understanding of the market, customer requirements, creating an awareness of the need for winning through quality, and implementation of improvements at all levels of the enterprise.

The enterprise's vision for enhancing value and excellence should be captured in a blueprint for continuous improvement that integrates quality and productivity improvement plans into the overall business strategy. Implementation elements should focus on empowering people for success and creating partnerships with customers and suppliers to continually improve products and services across the business units. The use of continuous improvement action teams to implement successful pilot projects is recommended. The results of the pilot projects should convince the enterprise team that success is built on the foundation of many small continuous improvement blocks that support the winning enterprise. The enterprise's leadership should make continuous improvement in quality, productivity, and total customer satisfaction an integral part of all enterprise activities, audit results, and revitalize improvement strategies.

Becoming a winning customer- and market-driven enterprise requires commitment to excellence and hard work. It involves setting the right improvement goals and objectives, as well as leveraging all resources and business assets by continuous improvement of all work processes and functions. It requires managing all product and service requirements from concept to commercialization. The strategic economic wars of the next several decades will center around winning through quality. Enterprises that will survive and win the war are those that are committed to continuous implementation of the ideas presented in this book. The benefits of continuous investment in ongoing projects include satisfying the customer, who is the ultimate judge of whether the price, delivery, and quality of goods and services are satisfactory; reduced development cost for products; increased market share and profitability; and improved job security and competitiveness.

Appendices

APPENDIX A

Case Studies

The objective of this section is to provide real-world examples of how some of the tools, techniques, and models presented in this book have been used to solve quality and productivity problems in various environments. The selected case studies cover both manufacturing and nonmanufacturing environments, process- and nonprocess-related problems, qualitative and quantitative methods, and resolution strategies.

Two case studies are provided in this section. In case study one, a custom systems engineering firm providing integrated turnkey computer systems to financial institutions has quality and reliability problems involving one key customer. In case study two, a purchasing department in a hospital is failing to provide quality services to internal operating departments.

Each case study includes the following:

- Case overview

- Case background

- Problem-resolution process

- Analysis and problem-resolution tools

- Process flow information

- Samples of tools used

Review the case studies to improve your understanding of the concepts, tools, and resolution approaches. Take time to consider the applicability of each case study to your environment.

191

Case Study One: Custom Systems, Inc.

A custom systems engineering firm providing integrated turnkey computer systems to financial institutions has quality and reliability problems involving one key customer.

Case Overview

CM Bank is one of Custom Systems' largest customers. Custom Systems has installed a networked automated teller machine (ATM) system at 7000 locations in the Northeast. Four regional nodes service approximately 1000 ATMs each, and there is a central office at the headquarters in New York City. The system had been in place for eight months when, within one month, complaints from ATM users increased by 64 percent. ATM downtime reports were up 48 percent. The problem had risen to the CEO level in both companies, with no resolution in sight. Efforts to resolve the problem were fragmented and ineffective.

Case Background

- Custom Systems designs, develops, and manufacturers custom computer systems.

- Most of the system hardware is off-the-shelf, requiring only minor modification and integration.

- Software is developed in-house.

- The hardware was purchased from over 80 suppliers.

- CM Bank has begun an in-house total quality program and has requested its suppliers to do likewise.

- Company processes have recently been modified without supplier or customer participation.

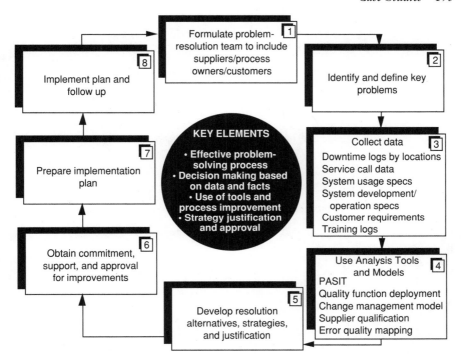

Figure A.1: Problem Resolution Process

Tool used	Purpose and process
Production and service improvement technique (PASIT)	Custom Systems realized that a "quick fix" resolution was not the key; long-term problem resolution and improvement in quality of products and services were required. A PASIT team was developed and authorized to investigate and improve the whole product-development and service process if necessary to resolve the problem at the source. The team consisted of representatives from key processes, suppliers, and customer representatives. The process was outlined in a flowchart, a simple version is shown in Figure A.4. Problems identified in the development process included • Knowledge of and attention to customer requirements up front were lacking. • Teamwork and integration of hardware and software efforts were nonexistent. • Process included too many inspections and sign-offs, thus obscuring lines of responsibility for quality, creating bottlenecks, and delaying schedules. • Delays led to the final product being released with known reliability problems.
Quality error mapping	Quality error mapping was used to analyze ATM downtime by location, service center, software patches employed, and hardware manufacturers of products used in the system. This analysis identified a peculiar set of hardware component issues.
Pareto analysis	Pareto analysis was used to prioritize component issues and led to the discovery of a unique combination of components that were used in 60 percent of the defective units
Cause-and-effect diagrams	Cause-and-effect diagrams were used to analyze the root cause of hardware failures and led to the isolation of a component and then a particular supplier.

Figure A.2: Analysis and Problem Resolution

Tool used	Purpose and process
Statistical process control	The suspect supplier's manufacturing process was analyzed using statistical process control charts. Supplier problems were identified and narrowed to specific processes within the supplier plant for correction.
Quality function deployment	The real source of the problem was a unique customer requirement that was overlooked by a key supplier and therefore not incorporated in the component supplied. A tailored QFD education program was implemented at the supplier and process-owner levels to ensure that this type of problem would not recur.
Process improvement	The PASIT team discovered that the lack of incorporation of a key customer requirement was pointed out at two different inspection steps during the development and production process, but no one took responsibility for correcting the problem. The PASIT team streamlined the development process to reduce the number of testing steps and external audits, and instituted a program of concurrent engineering (customer/supplier/process owner) teams during development.
TQM and change management model	The TQM and continuous improvement effort in place was having limited success due to the lack of attention to training the management team in teamwork concepts and how to manage change. As a result, many managers were pointing fingers and resisting the improvements that other managers were trying to make. A small group of managers had therefore decided to make changes they felt were required without gaining consensus. A training program was instituted to address these issues.
Supplier qualification	Many supplier quality issues were discovered during the analysis of the problem. As a result, a supplier education and qualification program was put in place.

Figure A.3: Analysis and Problem Resolution

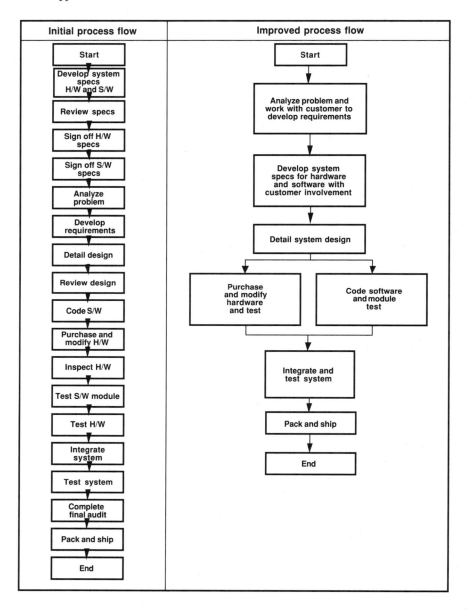

Figure A.4: Process Flow Diagram

PROBLEM SOURCE OR TYPE	LOCATION				TOTAL BY PROBLEM SOURCE OR TYPE
	NEW YORK / NEW JERSEY	PENNSYLVANIA	DC METROPOLITAN	MASSACHUSETTS/ RHODE ISLAND	
Hardware E1	8	9	6	12	35
Software E2	1	1	2	1	5
Environment E3	3	0	2	2	7
Personnel E4	1	1	0	5	7
Total Error ET by Location	13	11	10	20	54

Figure A.5: Sample of Quality Error Mapping Analysis

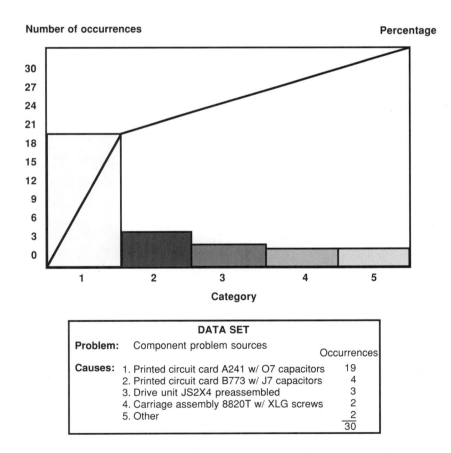

Figure A.6: Sample of Pareto Analysis

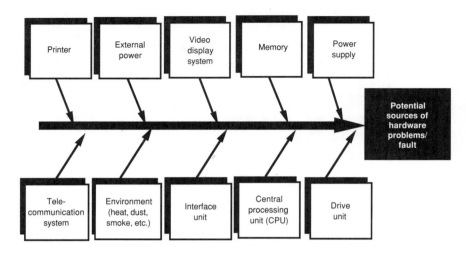

Figure A.7: Sample of Cause-and-Effect Analysis

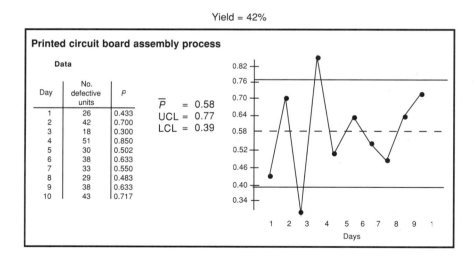

Figure A.8: Sample of Statistical Process Control Analysis

Case Study Two: Well Hospital Purchasing Department

A purchasing department in a hospital is failing to provide quality services to internal operating departments.

Case Overview

Well Hospital has a central purchasing organization responsible for supplying all operational units with equipment, tools, linens, pharmaceuticals, and other supplies. Complaints are mounting from internal organizations regarding turnaround time for order processing. According to recorded complaints, the purchasing process is inefficient and does not yield high-quality, high-value products and services. Managers report problems such as lost orders, incomplete orders, and wrong items being received.

Case Background

- Purchasing was centralized six months ago for cost reduction purposes.

- The purchasing department is responsible for negotiating for quality and price, but purchases are charged to other organizations' budgets.

- No measures have been put in place to evaluate the success of the centralized purchasing strategy or to measure quality and productivity of the new department.

- The new purchasing department is staffed with employees who previously handled purchasing for their respective departments. Though the function was centralized, the processes had not been standardized.

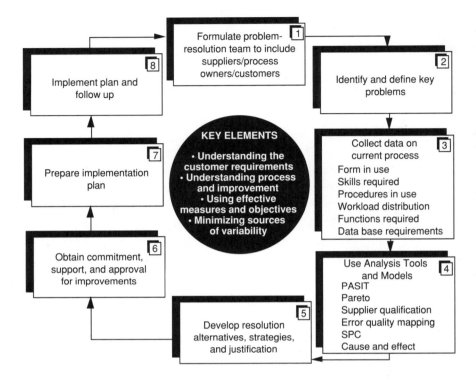

Figure A.9: Problem-Resolution Process

Tool used	Purpose and process
Production and service improvement technique (PASIT)	A team was developed and authorized to investigate the source of purchasing problems and to integrate the new department into an efficient, functioning team. The team consisted of department employees (process owners), representatives from key internal customers, a representative from the patient care review board, and a few key suppliers. The process was outlined in a flowchart. A simple version is shown in Figure A.11. Problems identified in the purchasing process included • No measures were in place. • No standard forms. • Management sign-off was a bottleneck. • No one was responsible for vendor/supplier responsiveness. • No process was in place for evaluating vendors and quotes to ensure high-quality/high-value selections. • No process was in place for evaluating internal customer satisfaction with products and services purchased.
SPC	The purchasing process cycle time was determined and evaluated for level of variability. This baselining of the current process allowed objectives and measures for improvement to be defined.
Cause-and-effect analysis	Cause-and-effect analysis was used to determine sources and root causes of variability.
Pareto analysis	Pareto analysis was used to prioritize the potential sources of variability and determine which areas to attack.

Figure A.10: Analysis and Problem Resolution

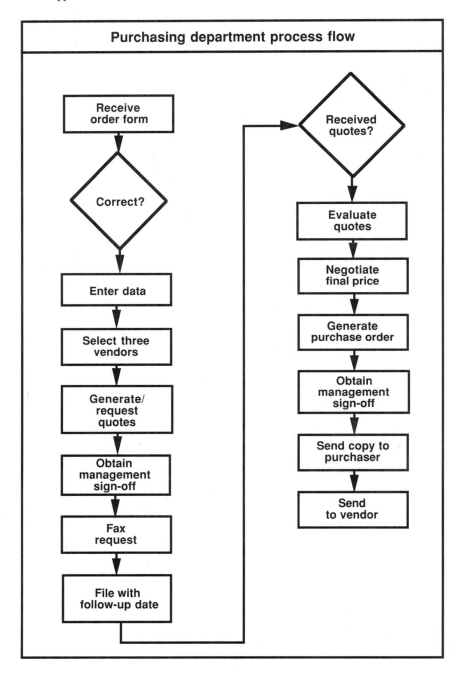

Figure A.11: Process Flowchart

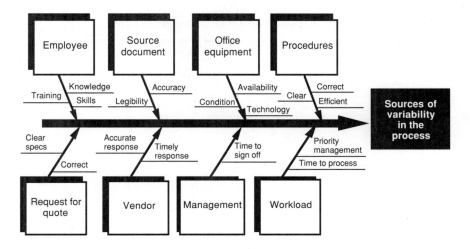

Figure A.12: Sample Cause-and-Effect Diagram

Number of occurrences

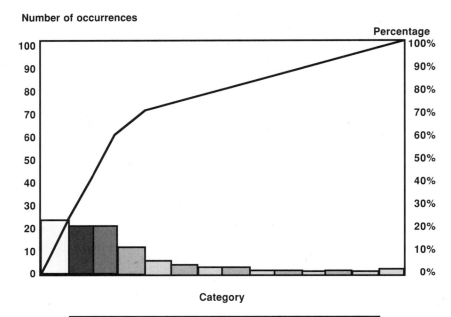

Category

Data set		
Problem: Excessive order processing time		
Causes:	Occurrences	Cumulative %
1. Source document illegible	23	23
2. Employee skills training	19	42
3. Procedures incorrect/nonexistent	19	61
4. Inaccurate vendor response	12	73
5. Office equipment down	5	78
6. Inaccurate spec to vendor	4	82
7. Management sign-off delay	3	85
8. Misplaced file	3	88
9. Procedures unclear	2	90
10. Office equipment not available	2	92
11. Mistake on request for quote	2	94
12. Source document incorrect	1	95
13. Vendor response late	1	96
14. Employee process knowledge	1	97
15. Other	3	100

Figure A.13: Sample Pareto Analysis

Tool used	Purpose and process
Quality error mapping	Quality error mapping was used to determine the sources of errors in incoming purchase orders.
Process improvement cycle	The following key measures were put in place. • Cycle time • Accuracy • Total quantity of orders processed • Pricing negotiation effectiveness • Quality of vendor selection • Process improvements A data base of acceptable pricing structures and strategies was developed. Training in negotiation was initiated for purchasing clerks. Sign-off authority for 80 percent of the purchase orders was given to purchasing clerks after training and certification in negotiating skills, cost management, and decision making.
Customer satisfaction measurement	The customers of the purchasing department were identified with the following key quality and productivity indicators. • Vendors — *Quality/clarity of quote requests, specifications, and all other correspondence including billing* • Operating departments • Management — *Quality/price and value of products and services purchased, processing time, and efficiency and responsiveness during all interaction and correspondence* • Patients • Other team members — *Teamwork and personal productivity* • Self-unit Measures included in-process checklists and surveys, customer feedback forums, team evaluations, and customer involvement in performance reviews.
Supplier Qualification	A supplier qualification and review data base was initiated and a feedback loop was put in place to ensure end user satisfaction with the quality and value of products and services.

Figure A.14: Analysis and Problem Resolution

Problem reason code	Organizations submitting purchase orders					
	Org 1	**Org 2**	**Org 3**	**Org 4**	**Org 5**	**Total**
Handwriting E1	5	3	0	1	3	12
Used wrong form E2	6	1	1	1	4	13
Instruction form missing E3	4	0	2	2	1	9
Employee error E4	1	1	7	1	0	10
Total errors ET	16	5	10	5	8	44

Figure A.15: Sample Quality Error Mapping Analysis

APPENDIX B

Exercises

1. Outline key requirements for becoming a customer- and market-driven enterprise.

2. Why are companies interested in becoming market driven?

3. Define a *customer- and market-driven enterprise, quality*, and *productivity*.

4. What does the term *total customer satisfaction* mean?

5. Discuss the strategies for coping with dynamic changes in the marketplace.

6. What are the difficulties involved in implementing the market-driven winning principles?

7. What is the impact of quality on market share and profitability?

8. Discuss six focus elements of a customer-oriented enterprise.

9. Outline the factors affecting productivity at the enterprise level.

10. Discuss the ten meanings of *quality*.

11. What are the advantages of having customer- and market-driven quality and productivity technologies?

12. Discuss the connection between quality, productivity, and total customer satisfaction.

13. Outline external challenges that could affect an enterprise's competitive position.

14. Define *input, process,* and *output optimization.*

15. What are the major differences between product and service quality?

16. Discuss typical errors that could affect quality in the work environment.

17. Why is it important to improve the quality of management and supervision?

18. Define *personal quality.* How can personal quality be improved?

19. What are driving forces for becoming a customer- and market-driven enterprise?

20. What are the goals of a customer- and market-driven enterprise? Discuss some of the key programs for achieving the goals.

21. Why is top management support important for the success of a quality program?

22. What is meant by *continuous improvement?*

23. What is meant by *management with facts and data?*

24. How should an enterprise focus on total customer satisfaction?

25. Is quality free? Why or why not?

26. Is six-sigma quality achievable? Why or why not?

27. Identify the key elements presented in the Edosomwan customer- and market-driven enterprise model.

28. Discuss key strategies for creating customer awareness and encouraging total participation in a continuous quality improvement program.

29. Outline a step-by-step procedure for creating a participative work environment.

30. Outline the content of a quality and productivity plan.

31. Outline the elements of a customer- and market-driven quality strategy.

32. What is meant by *error prevention* and *quality and productivity at the source?*

33. Determine the trial control limits and centerline for a percentage chart from the following data.

Number of subgroup inspections	20
Subgroup size	60
Total number of defectives	420

34. Given a standardized value of $\bar{p}$ = 0.10 and the following data from ten subgroups, determine whether the process is in control.

Subgroup	Subgroup Size	No. of Defectives
1	300	24
2	350	38
3	325	38
4	300	28
5	300	28
6	275	20
7	300	28
8	350	28
9	300	39
10	328	50

35. Determine trial control limits and the centerline for a C chart from the following data.

Number of subgroups	36
Number of units per subgroup	10
Total number of defects	800

36. Determine the trial control limits and the centerline for a C chart from the following data.

Number of subgroups	30
Number of units per subgroup	4
Total number of defects	300

37. Define *trial control limits.*

38. Explain the difference between variable and attribute control charts.

39. Is there a relationship between quality measurement and planning?

40. Define *normal variation.*

41. What are the advantages of a computer-assisted statistical process control data base?

42. Outline the ten principles for continuous improvement.

43. What does understanding the market mean to a process owner? Supplier? Customer?

44. Identify the key elements involved in market analysis and segmentation.

45. Why is it important to provide employees with the education required for the job?

46. Define *participative management, empowerment, workstation ownership,* and *entrepreneurship.*

47. Why is teamwork important in total quality management?

48. Why do people resist change?

49. Outline the strategies for creating a total quality culture.

50. Outline the strategies for preparing the enterprise team for change.

51. What are the procedures for helping business people manage change?

52. Identify the sources of resistance to change.

53. Outline the strategies for handling resistance to change at the operational unit level.

54. Define *change agent.*

55. How can change agent and transition structures be developed?

56. Why should change be implemented through manageable and familiar steps?

57. Define *resentment to a quality culture.*

58. What are the typical elements of a quality culture?

59. Outline the strategies for creating a total quality culture.

60. Define top management's role in creating a total quality culture.

61. What are the seven factors that top management must become concerned with in developing a quality improvement program?

62. Define *the quality blueprint.*

63. Outline the elements of a total quality culture and productivity management.

64. Outline strategies for making the transition to a new error-prevention quality philosophy.

65. What are the symptoms of a total quality culture?

66. Define *market-driven leader, market-driven manager,* and *market-driven employees.*

67. What are the characteristics of customer- and market-driven leaders and managers?

68. Describe techniques for improving the quality of management.

69. What are the key managerial and supervisory attributes for total productivity and quality management?

70. Discuss techniques for developing customer- and market-driven professionals and managers.

71. Is quality knowledge free?

72. Outline and discuss the eight directions for achieving managerial success.

73. Discuss the elements to be considered in getting quality products and services through people.

74. Outline the steps for correcting poor quality, productivity, and performance.

75. Discuss the four participative management skills.

76. Outline the elements that can foster teamwork.

77. Discuss strategies for motivating people to achieve quality and productivity excellence.

78. Define *quality function deployment.*

79. Outline the benefits of quality function deployment.

80. What are the problems involved in using quality function deployment?

81. Define *the voice of the customer.*

82. Define *the house of quality.*

83. Outline the requirements for implementing quality function deployment.

84. What are the responsibilities of top management in implementing quality function deployment?

85. Outline the potential practical problems with quality function deployment.

86. Outline key elements in the customer satisfaction model.

87. Discuss the four-step approach for improving total customer satisfaction.

88. Outline and discuss the five personal initiatives for achieving total customer satisfaction.

89. Define *dissatisfied customer, lost customer, valuable customer,* and *problematic customer.*

90. Define *six-sigma quality.*

91. What are the major differences between three- and six-sigma processes?

92. Identify the common sources of variation.

93. Discuss strategies for controlling variation.

94. Outline a step-by-step procedure for implementing a six-sigma process.

95. What are the major differences between attribute and variable control charts?

96. Outline the criteria for interpreting control charts.

97. What is meant when a process is described as "out of control"?

98. Define *assignable cause.* How can assignable cause be corrected in a production process?

99. Outline the rules for identifying a stable process.

100. What are the benefits of statistical process control?

101. Define *total quality management.*

102. Outline the steps for total quality management.

103. What is the meaning of *completed staff work?*

104. Outline the ten-step approach for problem solving.

105. What should be done when overwhelmed by a problem?

106. Discuss the process for facilitating problem solving.

107. What are the statistical uses of histograms? Pareto diagrams? Scatter diagrams? Run charts? Cost curves?

108. Outline the process for using the fishbone diagram.

109. Identify common sources and types of quality errors.

110. How can human errors be prevented?

111. How can quality errors be prevented through recognition and rewards?

112. Identify the essential elements of the quality error-prevention model.

113. Outline the six criteria for understanding human performance errors.

114. What are the major differences between the process-analysis matrix and the task-analysis matrix?

115. What are the difficulties involved in using the quality error-removal technique?

116. Identify the various quality costs and discuss strategies for controlling them.

117. Outline a step-by-step procedure for balancing productivity and quality requirements in the work environment.

118. Define the productivity and quality lever of balance.

119. What are common problems associated with implementing the productivity and quality evaluation procedure?

120. How can *underload* and *overload* affect quality and productivity?

121. What are the benefits of the productivity and quality assessment matrix?

122. Why should productivity and quality be managed together?

123. Outline the six steps for identifying excellent quality and productivity improvement projects.

124. Discuss the 9C principles for managing quality and productivity improvement projects.

125. Discuss four success factors for implementing total customer satisfaction.

126. What are the procedures for staying in touch with the customer?

127. Define *continuous measurable improvement with total customer satisfaction program*.

128. What are the factors behind successful quality and productivity projects?

129. Discuss the impact of technological innovation on quality, productivity, and competition.

130. Outline the procedure for market segmentation.

131. Identify the major sources of market requirements.

132. What is the key reason quality and productivity programs fail?

133. Discuss the role of teamwork in establishing quality and productivity objectives.

134. Identify common quality and productivity project implementation problems.

135. What is the meaning of *natural limits* in total quality management?

136. What are the characteristics of a successful market-driven enterprise?

137. Is zero defects achievable? Why or why not?

138. Outline the steps to be taken by the management team, employees, consultant, supplier, and process owner in a company interested in establishing a total customer satisfaction program.

139. What is the impact of poor employee morale on quality and productivity improvement?

140. How do the following affect the level of productivity and quality improvement?

    (a) Human resources

    (b) Management style

    (c) Recognition and reward

    (d) Workplace design and arrangement

    (e) Human factors and ergonomics

    (f) Employee attributes

    (g) Technology

    (h) Integrated systems (CIM, CAD/CAM)

    (i) Environmental safety

(j) Flexible work hours

(k) Company culture

(l) Computer data base

(m) Rules, regulations, and procedures

141. Estimate the mean and standard deviation of the insurance claims process from the observations listed below, which reflect defective claims. Also, estimate the process capability.

101	107	98	113	103
171	181	29	41	99
20	41	47	103	105
104	111	101	97	98

142. Find the capability limits of a toolmaking process which is normally distributed if the means and ranges of the subgroups of size 4 are as follows:

	Subgroup			
Chart	1	2	3	4
X	151	153	147	139
R	12	10	10	15

143. Determine the trial control limits and centerline for a *P* chart from the following data.

Number of subgroups inspected	30
Subgroup size	60
Total number of defectives	350

144. Assume that assignable causes have been found and eliminated for subgroups 30, 31, and 35. Compute revised control limits and the centerline using the remaining 35 observations.

145. Calculate the trail control limits and centerline of a percentage chart based on the following data obtained from a secretarial typing pool.

Number of subgroups inspected	45
Subgroup size	100
Total number of defectives	135

146. What is meant by *quality at the source* and *productivity at the source?* How is the quality that the customer sees defined?

147. Outline the steps that a general manager should follow to implement a productivity and quality program.

148. Define the terms *consumer's risk* and *producer's risk.* Why are inspection processes classified as non–value-adding operations?

149. Outline the steps that a general postmaster should follow to implement a productivity and quality program.

150. The defect rate of a clinical operation at Hoyer Hospital is 35 percent. The manager of the clinical operations says 25 percent of the defects are due to poor incoming materials. The supplier of the incoming materials believes its process is perfect. The hospital unit is losing 216 patients per day. Develop a comprehensive productivity and quality improvement process that will enable Hoyer Hospital to be competitive, reduce defect levels to zero, and regain patient confidence and business.

151. Explain how the morale and motivation level of individuals can affect productivity and quality.

152. Edosomwan proposes that 80 percent of productivity and quality errors that occur in the manufacturing and service work environments are due to management mistakes. Do you agree with this statement? Why or why not? Develop improvement strategies for minimizing management mistakes that affect the level of productivity growth and quality improvement.

153. Discuss senior management's major requirements when reviewing productivity and quality improvement projects.

154. A tough production manager wishes to reduce defect levels of television units by 15 percent, improve productivity by 35 percent, reduce work-in-process inventory by 10 percent, reduce manpower by 18 percent, and increase employee salaries by 20 percent per year. How can the manager achieve these apparently contradictory objectives?

155. How many different samples of size 5 can be obtained from a population of size 100? 505? 90?

156. Find the capability limits of a process which is approximately normally distributed if the means and ranges of subgroups of size 15 are as follows:

	Subgroup 1	Subgroup 2	Subgroup 3	Subgroup 4	Subgroup 5
x	0.576	0.832	1.004	0.968	0.888
R	0.007	0.009	0.016	0.014	0.009

157. Given the following frequency distribution,

Class	Frequency
3–17	4
18–22	7
23–27	9
28–32	4
33–37	1

   (a) What is the upper-class limit of the second class?
   (b) What is the lower-class limit of the third class?
   (c) What is the lower-class boundary of the third class?
   (d) What is the upper-class boundary of the second class?
   (e) What is the class mark of the fourth class?
   (f) What is the class interval of the distribution?

158. Discuss the Edosomwan market-driven principles for quality, productivity, and total customer satisfaction management. How should the principles be implemented in a manufacturing and service work environment?

159. Discuss the three types of customers and the strategies for handling customer complaints.

160. Identify the sources of resistance to change in organizations and outline strategies for overcoming them.

161. Define benchmarking and outline a step-by-step approach for benchmarking work processes.

162. Outline the key success factors for creating a total quality culture.

163. What are the key elements of a world-class, customer-driven organization?

Malcolm Baldrige National Quality Award Criteria

1993 Examination categories/items	Points (total 1000)	Key indicators
1.0 Leadership **(95 points)**		*Leadership trained on continuous improvement and practicing principles, tools, and techniques*
1.1 Senior executive leadership	45	
1.2 Management for quality	25	
1.3 Public responsibility and corporate citizenship	25	
2.0 Information and analysis **(75 points)**		*Decision making based on facts and analysis rather than gut feel*
2.1 Scope and management of quality and performance data and information	15	
2.2 Competitive comparisons and benchmarking	20	
2.3 Analysis and uses of company-level data	40	
3.0 Strategic quality planning **(60 points)**		*Planning and goal setting at all levels to ensure alignment with corporate strategic plan; proactive, not reactive, management*
3.1 Strategic quality and company performance planning process	35	
3.2 Quality and performance plans	25	
4.0 Human resource development and management **(150 points)**		*Practices and policies that recognize the human resources as the most valuable resource and development as the key*
4.1 Human resource planning and management	20	
4.2 Employee involvement	40	
4.3 Employee education and training	40	
4.4 Employee performance and recognition	25	
4.5 Employee well-being and satisfaction	25	
5.0 Management of process quality **(140 points)**		*Focus is on measuring, managing, and ensuring internal and external quality at the source of product or service production*
5.1 Design and introduction of quality products and services	40	
5.2 Process management: product and service production and delivery processes	35	
5.3 Process management: business processes and support services	30	
5.4 Supplier quality	20	
5.5 Quality assessment	15	
6.0 Quality and operational results **(180 points)**		*Long-term and short-term trends show commitment, progress, and success in the journey*
6.1 Product and service quality results	70	
6.2 Company operational results	50	
6.3 Business process and support service results	25	
6.4 Supplier quality results	35	
7.0 Customer focus and satisfaction **(300 points)**		*Focus is on understanding the needs, wants, and desires of the internal, external, and self-unit customer*
7.1 Customer expectations: current and future	35	
7.2 Customer relationship management	65	
7.3 Commitment to customers	15	
7.4 Customer satisfaction determination	30	
7.5 Customer satisfaction results	85	
7.6 Customer satisfaction comparison	70	

APPENDIX D

Statistical Tables

Standard Normal Distribution
(Area Under Normal Curve)

a = the proportion of process output beyond a particular value of interest (such as a specification limit) that is z standard deviation units away from the process average (for a process that is in statistical control and is normally distributed). For example, if z = 2.17, a = .0150 or 1.5%. In any actual situation, this proportion is only approximate.

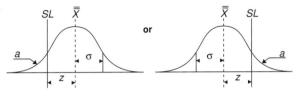

|z|	x.x0	x.x1	x.x2	x.x3	x.x4	x.x5	x.x6	x.x7	x.x8	x.x9
4.0	.00003									
3.9	.00005	.00005	.00004	.00004	.00004	.00004	.00004	.00004	.00003	.00003
3.8	.00007	.00007	.00007	.00006	.00006	.00006	.00006	.00005	.00005	.00005
3.7	.00011	.00010	.00010	.00010	.00009	.00009	.00008	.00008	.00008	.00008
3.6	.00016	.00015	.00015	.00014	.00014	.00013	.00013	.00012	.00012	.00011
3.5	.00023	.00022	.00022	.00021	.00020	.00019	.00019	.00018	.00017	.00017
3.4	.00034	.00032	.00031	.00030	.00029	.00028	.00027	.00026	.00025	.00024
3.3	.00048	.00047	.00045	.00043	.00042	.00040	.00039	.00038	.00036	.00035
3.2	.00069	.00066	.00064	.00062	.00060	.00058	.00056	.00054	.00052	.00050
3.1	.00097	.00094	.00090	.00087	.00084	.00082	.00079	.00076	.00074	.00071
3.0	.00135	.00131	.00126	.00122	.00118	.00114	.00111	.00107	.00104	.00100
2.9	.0019	.0018	.0018	.0017	.0016	.0016	.0015	.0015	.0014	.0014
2.8	.0026	.0025	.0024	.0023	.0023	.0022	.0021	.0021	.0020	.0019
2.7	.0035	.0034	.0033	.0032	.0031	.0030	.0029	.0028	.0027	.0026
2.6	.0047	.0045	.0044	.0043	.0041	.0040	.0039	.0038	.0037	.0036
2.5	.0062	.0060	.0059	.0057	.0055	.0054	.0052	.0051	.0049	.0048
2.4	.0082	.0080	.0078	.0075	.0073	.0071	.0069	.0068	.0066	.0064
2.3	.0107	.0104	.0120	.0099	.0096	.0094	.0091	.0089	.0087	.0084
2.2	.0139	.0136	.0132	.0129	.0125	.0122	.0119	.0116	.0113	.0110
2.1	.0179	.0174	.0170	.0166	.0162	.0158	.0154	.0150	.0146	.0143
2.0	.0228	.0222	.0217	.0212.	.0207	.0202	.0197	.0192	.0188	.0183
1.9	.0287	.0281	.0274	.0268	.0262	.0256	.0250	.0244	.0239	.0233
1.8	.0359	.0351	.0344	.0336	.0329	.0322	.0314	.0307	.0301	.0294
1.7	.0446	.0436	.0427	.0418	.0409	.0401	.0392	.0384	.0375	.0367
1.6	.0548	.0537	.0526	.0516	.0505	.0495	.0485	.0475	.0465	.0455
1.5	.0668	.0655	.0643	.0630	.0618	.0606	.0594	.0582	.0571	.0559
1.4	.0808	.0793	.0778	.0764	.0749	.0735	.0721	.0708	.0694	.0681
1.3	.0968	.0951	.0934	.0918	.0901	.0885	.0869	.0853	.0838	.0823
1.2	.1151	.1131	.1112	.1093	.1075	.1056	.1038	.1020	.1003	.0985
1.1	.1357	.1335	.1314	.1292	.1271	.1251	.1230	.1210	.1190	.1170
1.0	.1587	.1562	.1539	.1515	.1492	.1469	.1446	.1423	.1401	.1379
0.9	.1841	.1814	.1788	.1762	.1736	.1711	.1685	.1660	.1635	.1161
0.8	.2119	.2090	.2061	.2033	.2005	.1977	.1949	.1922	.1894	.1867
0.7	.2420	.2389	.2358	.2327	.2297	.2266	.2236	.2206	.2177	.2148
0.6	.2743	.2709	.2676	.2643	.2611	.2578	.2546	.2514	.2483	.2451
0.5	.3085	.3050	.3015	.2981	.2946	.2912	.2877	.2843	.2810	.2776
0.4	.3446	.3409	.3372	.3336	.3300	.3264	.3228	.3192	.3156	.3121
0.3	.3821	.3783	.3745	.3707	.3669	.3632	.3594	.3557	.3520	.3483
0.2	.4207	.4168	.4129	.4090	.4052	.4013	.3974	.3936	.3897	.3859
0.1	.4602	.4562	.4522	.4483	.4443	.4404	.4364	.4325	.4286	.4247
0.0	.5000	.4960	.4920	.4880	.4840	.4801	.4761	.4721	.4681	.4641

All statistical tables in Appendix D are reprinted with permission from Johnson A. Edosomwan, *Integrating Productivity and Quality Management*. New York: Marcel Dekker, 1987.

Figure D.1: Statistical Tables: Standard Normal Distribution

F-Distribution Table, α = 0.5

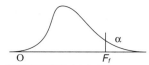

d.f.2	d.f.1 (numerator)							
(denominator)	1	2	3	4	5	6	7	8
1	161	200	216	225	230	234	237	239
2	18.5	19.0	19.2	19.2	19.3	19.3	19.4	19.4
3	10.1	9.55	9.28	9.12	9.01	8.94	8.89	8.85
4	7.71	6.94	6.59	6.39	6.26	6.16	6.09	6.04
5	6.61	5.79	5.41	5.19	5.05	4.95	4.88	4.82
6	5.99	5.14	4.76	4.53	4.39	4.28	4.21	4.15
7	5.59	4.74	4.35	4.12	3.97	3.87	3.79	3.73
8	5.32	4.46	4.07	3.84	3.69	3.58	3.50	3.44
9	5.12	4.26	3.86	3.63	3.48	3.37	3.29	3.23
10	4.96	4.10	3.71	3.48	3.33	3.22	3.14	3.07
11	4.84	3.98	3.59	3.36	3.20	3.09	3.01	2.95
12	4.75	3.89	3.49	3.26	3.11	3.00	2.91	2.85
13	4.67	3.81	3.41	3.18	3.03	2.92	2.83	2.77
14	4.60	3.74	3.34	3.11	2.96	2.85	2.76	2.70
15	4.54	3.68	3.29	3.06	2.90	2.79	2.71	2.64
16	4.49	3.63	3.24	3.01	2.85	2.74	2.66	2.59
17	4.45	3.59	3.20	2.96	2.81	2.70	2.61	2.55
18	4.41	3.55	3.16	2.93	2.77	2.66	2.58	2.51
19	4.38	3.52	3.13	2.90	2.74	2.63	2.54	2.48
20	4.35	3.49	3.10	2.87	2.71	2.60	2.51	2.45
21	4.32	3.47	3.07	2.84	2.68	2.57	2.49	2.42
22	4.30	3.44	3.05	2.82	2.66	2.55	2.46	2.40
23	4.28	3.42	3.03	2.80	2.64	2.53	2.44	2.37
24	4.26	3.40	3.01	2.78	2.62	2.51	2.42	2.36
25	4.24	3.39	2.99	2.76	2.60	2.49	2.40	2.34
30	4.17	3.32	2.92	2.69	2.53	2.42	2.33	2.27
40	4.08	3.23	2.84	2.61	2.45	2.34	2.25	2.18
60	4.00	3.15	2.76	2.53	2.37	2.25	2.17	2.10
120	3.92	3.07	2.68	2.45	2.29	2.18	2.09	2.02
∞	3.84	3.00	2.60	2.37	2.21	2.10	2.01	1.94

d.f.1 (numerator)										
9	10	12	15	20	24	30	40	60	120	x
241	242	244	246	248	249	250	251	252	253	254
19.4	19.4	19.4	19.4	19.4	19.5	19.5	19.5	19.5	19.5	19.5
8.81	8.79	8.74	8.70	8.66	8.64	8.62	8.59	8.57	8.55	8.53
6.00	5.96	5.91	5.86	5.80	5.77	5.75	5.72	5.69	5.66	5.63
4.77	4.74	4.68	4.62	4.56	4.53	4.50	4.46	4.43	4.40	4.37
4.10	4.06	4.00	3.94	3.87	3.84	3.81	3.77	3.74	3.70	3.67
3.68	3.64	3.57	3.51	3.44	3.41	3.38	3.34	3.30	3.27	3.23
3.39	3.35	3.28	3.22	3.15	3.12	3.08	3.04	3.01	2.97	2.93
3.18	3.14	3.07	3.01	2.94	2.90	2.86	2.83	2.79	2.75	2.71
3.02	2.98	2.91	2.85	2.77	2.74	2.70	2.66	2.62	2.58	2.54
2.90	2.85	2.79	2.72	2.65	2.61	2.57	2.53	2.49	2.45	2.40
2.80	2.75	2.69	2.62	2.54	2.51	2.47	2.43	2.38	2.34	2.30
2.71	2.67	2.60	2.53	2.46	2.42	2.38	2.34	2.30	2.25	2.21
2.65	2.60	2.53	2.46	2.39	2.35	2.31	2.27	2.22	2.18	2.13
2.59	2.54	2.48	2.40	2.33	2.29	2.25	2.20	2.16	2.11	2.07
2.54	2.49	2.42	2.35	2.28	2.24	2.19	2.15	2.11	2.06	2.01
2.49	2.45	2.38	2.31	2.23	2.19	2.15	2.10	2.06	2.01	1.96
2.46	2.41	2.34	2.27	2.19	2.15	2.11	2.06	2.02	1.97	1.92
2.42	2.38	2.31	2.23	2.16	2.11	2.07	2.03	1.98	1.93	1.88
2.39	2.35	2.28	2.20	2.12	2.08	2.04	1.99	1.95	1.90	1.84
2.37	2.32	2.25	2.18	2.10	2.05	2.01	1.96	1.92	1.87	1.81
2.34	2.30	2.23	2.15	2.07	2.03	1.98	1.94	1.89	1.84	1.78
2.32	2.27	2.20	2.13	2.05	2.01	1.96	1.91	1.86	1.81	1.76
2.30	2.25	2.18	2.11	2.03	1.98	1.94	1.89	1.84	1.79	1.73
2.28	2.24	2.16	2.09	2.01	1.96	1.92	1.87	1.82	1.77	1.71
2.21	2.16	2.09	2.01	1.93	1.89	1.84	1.79	1.74	1.68	1.62
2.12	2.08	2.00	1.92	1.84	1.79	1.74	1.69	1.64	1.58	1.51
2.04	1.99	1.92	1.84	1.75	1.70	1.65	1.59	1.53	1.47	1.39
1.96	1.91	1.83	1.75	1.66	1.61	1.55	1.50	1.43	1.35	1.25
1.88	1.83	1.75	1.67	1.57	1.52	1.46	1.39	1.32	1.22	1.00

Figure D.2: Statistical Tables: F-Distribution Table

F-Distribution Table, α = 0.1

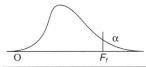

d.f.2 (denominator)	d.f.1 (numerator)							
	1	2	3	4	5	6	7	8
1	4.052	5.000	5.403	5.625	5.764	5.859	5.928	5.982
2	98.5	99.0	99.2	99.2	99.3	99.3	99.4	99.4
3	34.1	30.8	29.5	28.7	28.2	27.9	27.7	27.5
4	21.2	18.0	16.7	16.0	15.5	15.2	15.0	14.8
5	16.3	13.3	12.1	11.4	11.0	10.7	10.5	10.3
6	13.7	10.9	9.78	9.15	8.75	8.47	8.26	8.10
7	12.2	9.55	8.45	7.85	7.46	7.19	6.99	6.84
8	11.3	8.65	7.59	7.01	6.63	6.37	6.18	6.03
9	10.6	8.02	6.99	6.42	6.06	5.80	5.61	5.47
10	10.0	7.56	6.55	5.99	5.64	5.39	5.20	5.06
11	9.65	7.21	6.22	5.67	5.32	5.07	4.89	4.74
12	9.33	6.93	5.95	5.41	5.06	4.82	4.64	4.50
13	9.07	6.70	5.74	5.21	4.86	4.62	4.44	4.30
14	8.86	6.51	5.56	5.04	4.70	4.46	4.28	4.14
15	8.68	6.36	5.42	4.89	4.56	4.32	4.14	4.00
16	8.53	6.23	5.29	4.77	4.44	4.20	4.03	3.89
17	8.40	6.11	5.19	4.67	4.34	4.10	3.93	3.79
18	8.29	6.01	5.09	4.58	4.25	4.01	3.84	3.71
19	8.19	5.93	5.01	4.50	4.17	3.94	3.77	3.63
20	8.10	5.85	4.94	4.43	4.10	3.87	3.70	3.56
21	8.02	5.78	4.87	4.37	4.04	3.81	3.64	3.51
22	7.95	5.72	4.82	4.31	3.99	3.76	3.59	3.45
23	7.88	5.66	4.76	4.26	3.94	3.71	3.54	3.41
24	7.82	5.61	4.72	4.22	3.90	3.67	3.50	3.36
25	7.77	5.57	4.68	4.18	3.86	3.63	3.46	3.32
30	7.56	5.39	4.51	4.02	3.70	3.47	3.30	3.17
40	7.31	5.18	4.31	3.83	3.51	3.29	3.12	2.99
60	7.08	4.98	4.13	3.65	3.34	3.12	2.95	2.82
120	6.85	4.79	3.95	3.48	3.17	2.96	2.79	2.66
∞	6.63	4.61	3.78	3.32	3.02	2.80	2.64	2.51

	d.f.1 (numerator)									
9	10	12	15	20	24	30	40	60	120	x
6.023	6.056	6.106	6.157	6.209	6.235	6.261	6.287	6.313	6.339	6.366
99.4	99.4	99.4	99.4	99.4	99.5	99.5	99.5	99.5	99.5	99.5
27.3	27.2	27.1	26.9	26.7	26.6	26.5	26.4	26.3	26.2	26.1
14.7	14.5	14.4	14.2	14.0	13.9	13.8	13.7	13.7	13.6	13.5
10.2	10.1	9.89	9.72	9.55	9.47	9.38	9.29	9.20	9.11	9.02
7.98	7.87	7.72	7.56	7.40	7.31	7.23	7.14	7.06	6.97	6.88
6.72	6.62	6.47	6.31	6.16	6.07	5.99	5.91	5.82	5.74	5.65
5.91	5.81	5.67	5.52	5.36	5.28	5.20	5.12	5.03	4.95	4.86
5.35	5.26	5.11	4.96	4.81	4.73	4.65	4.57	4.48	4.40	4.31
4.94	4.85	4.71	4.56	4.41	4.33	4.25	4.17	4.08	4.00	3.91
4.63	4.54	4.40	4.25	4.10	4.02	3.94	3.86	3.78	3.69	3.60
4.39	4.30	4.16	4.01	3.86	3.78	3.70	3.62	3.54	3.45	3.36
4.19	4.10	3.96	3.82	3.66	3.59	3.51	3.43	3.34	3.25	3.17
4.03	3.94	3.80	3.66	3.51	3.43	3.35	3.27	3.18	3.09	3.00
3.89	3.80	3.67	3.52	3.37	3.29	3.21	3.13	3.05	2.96	2.87
3.78	3.69	3.55	3.41	3.26	3.18	3.10	3.02	2.93	2.84	2.75
3.68	3.59	3.46	3.31	3.16	3.08	3.00	2.92	2.83	2.75	2.65
3.60	3.51	3.37	3.23	3.08	3.00	2.92	2.84	2.75	2.66	2.57
3.52	3.43	3.30	3.15	3.00	2.92	2.84	2.76	2.67	2.58	2.49
3.46	3.37	3.23	3.09	2.94	2.86	2.78	2.69	2.61	2.52	2.42
3.40	3.31	3.17	3.03	2.88	2.80	2.72	2.64	2.55	2.46	2.36
3.35	3.26	3.12	2.98	2.83	2.75	2.67	2.58	2.50	2.40	2.31
3.30	3.21	3.07	2.93	2.78	2.70	2.62	2.54	2.45	2.35	2.26
3.26	3.17	3.03	2.89	2.74	2.66	2.58	2.49	2.40	2.31	2.21
3.22	3.13	2.99	2.85	2.70	2.62	2.53	2.45	2.36	2.27	2.17
3.07	2.98	2.84	2.70	2.55	2.47	2.39	2.30	2.21	2.11	2.01
2.89	2.80	2.66	2.52	2.37	2.29	2.20	2.11	2.02	1.92	1.80
2.72	2.63	2.50	2.35	2.20	2.12	2.03	1.94	1.84	1.73	1.60
2.56	2.47	2.34	2.19	2.03	1.95	1.86	1.76	1.66	1.53	1.38
2.41	2.32	2.18	2.04	1.88	1.79	1.70	1.59	1.47	1.32	1.00

Figure D.3: Statistical Tables: F-Distribution Table

t-Distribution Table

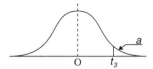

d.f.	t_{100}	t_{050}	t_{025}	t_{010}	t_{005}
1	3.078	6.314	12.706	31.821	63.657
2	1.886	2.920	4.303	6.965	9.925
3	1.638	2.353	3.182	4.541	5.841
4	1.533	2.132	2.776	3.747	4.604
5	1.476	2.015	2.571	3.365	4.032
6	1.440	1.943	2.447	3.143	3.707
7	1.415	1.895	2.365	2.998	3.499
8	1.397	1.860	2.306	2.896	3.355
9	1.383	1.833	2.262	2.821	3.250
10	1.372	1.812	2.228	2.764	3.169
11	1.363	1.796	2.201	2.718	3.106
12	1.356	1.782	2.179	2.681	3.055
13	1.350	1.771	2.160	2.650	3.012
14	1.345	1.761	2.145	2.624	2.977
15	1.341	1.753	2.131	2.602	2.947
16	1.337	1.746	2.120	2.583	2.921
17	1.333	1.740	2.110	2.567	2.898
18	1.330	1.734	2.101	2.552	2.878
19	1.328	1.729	2.093	2.539	2.861
20	1.325	1.725	2.086	2.528	2.845
21	1.323	1.721	2.080	2.518	2.831
22	1.321	1.717	2.074	2.508	2.819
23	1.319	1.714	2.069	2.500	2.807
24	1.318	1.711	2.064	2.492	2.797
25	1.316	1.708	2.060	2.485	2.787
26	1.315	1.706	2.056	2.479	2.779
27	1.314	1.703	2.052	2.473	2.771
28	1.313	1.701	2.048	2.467	2.763
29	1.311	1.699	2.045	2.462	2.756
∞	1.282	1.645	1.960	2.326	2.576

Figure D.4: Statistical Tables: t-Distribution Table

Control chart for attribute data calculation worksheet

Number

(Subgroup sizes must be equal.)

Nonconforming units

np Chart

$$\text{UCL } np, \text{ LCL } np = np \pm 3\sqrt{np\left(1 - \frac{np}{n}\right)}$$

Nonconformities

c Chart

$$\text{UCl } c, \text{ LCL } c = \bar{c} \pm 3\sqrt{\bar{c}}$$

Proportion

(Subgroup sizes need not be equal.)

p Chart

$$\text{UCL } p, \text{ LCL } p = \bar{p} \pm 3\sqrt{p\left(1 - \frac{\bar{p}}{n}\right)}$$

u Chart

$$\text{UCl } u, \text{ LCL } u = \bar{u} \pm 3\sqrt{\frac{\bar{u}}{n}}$$

p Chart

$$\text{or} = \bar{p} \pm 3\frac{\sqrt{\bar{p}(1 - \bar{p})}}{\sqrt{n}}$$

$$\text{or} = \bar{u} \pm 3\frac{\sqrt{\bar{u}}}{\sqrt{n}}$$

Notes: Record all adjustments, tool changes, etc.

Subgroup No.	Date	Time	Comments

Figure D.5: Calculation Worksheet for Attribute Control Charts

Variables control chart for individuals X and R _{Individuals and ranges} calculation worksheet

Preliminary control limits (based on subgroups:_____)	**Revised control limits** (if necessary)
Calculate average range:	
$R - \dfrac{\Sigma R}{k}$ _____ _____	$\bar{R} = $ _____ _____
Σ Sum of, and k number of subgroups	
Calculate control limits for ranges:	
UCL $D_4 \times \bar{R} = $ _____ × _____ _____	$UCL_{\bar{R}} = $ _____ × _____ _____
LCL $D_4 \times \bar{R} = $ _____ × _____ _____	$LCL_{\bar{R}} = $ _____ × _____ _____
Calculate process average:	
$X - \dfrac{\Sigma X}{k}$ _____ _____	X _____ _____
Calculate control limits for individuals:	
$E_4 \bar{R} = $ _____ × _____ _____	$E_4 \bar{R} = $ _____ × _____ _____
UCL $\bar{X} + E_4 \bar{R} = $ _____ × _____ _____	UCL = _____ × _____ _____
LCL $\bar{X} - E_4 \bar{R} = $ _____ × _____ _____	LCL = _____ × _____ _____
Estimate of standard deviation (if the process is in statistical control):	
$\sigma \ \dfrac{R}{d_2}$ _____	

Subgroup size					Subgroup size				
n	E_2	D_1	D_4	d_4	n	E_2	D_1	D_4	d_4
2	2.660	–	3.267	1.128	6	1.184	–	2.004	2.534
3	1.772	–	2.575	1.693	7	1.109	0.076	1.924	2.704
4	1.457	–	2.282	2.059	8	1.054	0.136	1.864	2.847
5	1.290	–	2.115	2.326	9	1.010	0.184	1.816	2.970
					10	0.975	0.223	1.777	3.078

*Lower control limits for *R* do not exist for sample sizes below 7

Notes: Record all adjustments, tool changes, etc.

Subgroup no.	Date	Time	Comments

Figure D.6: Calculation Worksheet for Variable Control Charts

Measurement system/gage capability calculation worksheet

Part asm. name	Gage name	Part no.
Characteristic	Gage no.	Measurement unit
Specification	Gage type	Zero equals

Operator	A				B				C			
Sample no.	1st trial	2nd trial	3rd trial	Range	1st trial	2nd trial	3rd trial	Range	1st trial	2nd trial	3rd trial	Range
1												
2												
3												
4												
5												
6												
7												
8												
9												
10												
Totals												

$\bar{R}$ $\bar{R}$ $\bar{R}$

Sum $\bar{X}$ Sum $\bar{X}$ Sum $\bar{X}$

Test for control:

Upper control limit, UCL $= D_4\bar{R} =$ _____ $\times$ _____ _____

where: R is the average of $\bar{R} + \bar{R} + \bar{R} =$ _____ _____ _____ _____ _____

     $D_4 = 3.28$ for 2 trials or 2.58 for 3 trials.

If any individual range exceeds this limit, the measurement or reading should be reviewed. repeated, corrected or discarded as appropriate, and new averages and ranges should be computed.

Measurement system gage capability analysis:

Equipment variation ("repeatability") $K_1\bar{R}$ _____ $\times$ _____ [_____] Repeatability

where: $K_1 = 4.56$ for 2 trials or 3.05 for 3 trials.

Operator variation ("reproductibility") $K_2\bar{X}$ _____ $\times$ _____ [_____] Reproducibility

where: $K_2 = 3.56$ for 2 operators or 2.70 for 3 operators.

X is the difference between the max. and min.

Total "repeatability" and "reproducibility" variation (R&R) $\sqrt{\text{(Repeatability)} + \text{(Reproducibility)}}$

Gage capability

$\sqrt{(\underline{\hspace{2cm}}) + (\underline{\hspace{2cm}})}$ $\sqrt{\underline{\hspace{1cm}} + \underline{\hspace{1cm}}}$ $\sqrt{\underline{\hspace{1cm}}}$ [_____]

Gage acceptability determination: $\dfrac{\text{Total gage capability (R\&R)}}{\text{Specification tolerance}}$ _____   [_____] %

Notes

_____

_____

_____

_____

_____

Analysis performed by:	Date:

Figure D.7: Calculation Worksheet for Gage Capability

X̄ and R, X̄ and S charts

	X̄ and R charts*				X̄ and S charts*			
	Chart for averages (X̄)	Chart for ranges (R)			Chart for averages (X̄)	Chart for standard deviation (s)		
	Factors for control limits	Divisors for estimate of standard deviation	Factors for control limits		Factors for control limits	Divisors for estimate of standard deviation	Factors for control limits	
Subgroup size n	A_2	d_2	D_3	D_4	A_3	c_4	B_3	B_4
2	1.880	1.128	—	3.267	2.659	0.7979	—	3.267
3	1.023	1.693	—	2.574	1.954	0.8862	—	2.568
4	0.729	2.059	—	2.282	1.628	0.9213	—	2.266
5	0.577	2.326	—	2.114	1.427	0.9400	—	2.089
6	0.483	2.534	—	2.004	1.287	0.9515	0.030	1.970
7	0.419	2.704	0.076	1.924	1.182	0.9594	0.118	1.882
8	0.373	2.847	0.136	1.864	1.099	0.9650	0.185	1.815
9	0.337	2.970	0.184	1.816	1.032	0.9693	0.239	1.761
10	0.308	3.078	0.223	1.777	0.975	0.9727	0.284	1.716
11	0.285	3.173	0.256	1.744	0.927	0.9754	0.321	1.679
12	0.266	3.258	0.283	1.717	0.886	0.9776	0.354	1.646
13	0.249	3.336	0.307	1.693	0.850	0.9794	0.382	1.618
14	0.235	3.407	0.328	1.672	0.817	0.9810	0.406	1.594
15	0.223	3.472	0.347	1.653	0.789	0.9823	0.428	1.572
16	0.212	3.532	0.363	1.637	0.763	0.9835	0.448	1.552
17	0.203	3.588	0.378	1.622	0.739	0.9845	0.466	1.534
18	0.194	3.640	0.391	1.608	0.718	0.9854	0.482	1.518
19	0.187	3.689	0.403	1.597	0.698	0.9862	0.497	1.503
20	0.180	3.735	0.415	1.585	0.680	0.9869	0.510	1.490
21	0.173	3.778	0.425	1.575	0.663	0.9876	0.523	1.477
22	0.167	3.819	0.434	1.566	0.647	0.9882	0.534	1.466
23	0.162	3.858	0.443	1.557	0.633	0.9887	0.545	1.455
24	0.157	3.895	0.451	1.548	0.619	0.9892	0.555	1.445
25	0.153	3.931	0.459	1.541	0.606	0.9896	0.565	1.435

$$UCL_{\bar{X}} + LCL_{\bar{X}} = \bar{X} \pm A_2\bar{R}$$
$$UCL_R = D_4\bar{R}$$
$$LCL_R = D_3\bar{R}$$
$$\alpha = \bar{R}/d_2$$

$$UCL_{\bar{X}} + LCL_{\bar{X}} = \bar{X} \pm A_3\bar{S}$$
$$UCL_{\bar{S}} = B_4\bar{S}$$
$$LCL_{\bar{S}} = B_3\bar{S}$$
$$\alpha = \bar{S}/c_4$$

*From ASTM publication STP-45D. *Manual on the Presentation of Data and Control Chart Analysis.* 1976: pp. 134–136. Copyright ASTM. 1916 Race Street, Philadelphia, Penn. 19103. Reprinted with permission.

Figure D.8: Statistical Tables: X̄, R, X̄, and S Charts

Medial and Individual Charts

	Median charts**				Charts for individuals*			
	Charts for medians ($\tilde{X}$)	Chart for ranges (R)			Charts for individuals (X)	Chart for ranges (R)		
	Factors for control limits	Divisors for estimate of standard deviation	Factors for control limits		Factors for control limits	Divisors for estimate of standard deviation	Factors for control limits	
Subgroup size	A_2	d_2	D_3	D_4	E_2	d_2	D_3	D_4
2	1.880	1.128	—	3.267	2.660	1.128	—	3.267
3	1.187	1.693	—	2.574	1.772	1.693	—	2.574
4	0.796	2.059	—	2.282	1.457	2.059	—	2.282
5	0.691	2.326	—	2.114	1.290	2.326	—	2.114
6	0.548	2.534	—	2.004	1.184	2.534	—	2.004
7	0.508	2.704	0.076	1.924	1.109	2.704	0.076	1.924
8	0.433	2.847	0.136	1.864	1.054	2.847	0.136	1.864
9	0.412	2.970	0.184	1.816	1.010	2.970	0.184	1.816
10	0.362	3.078	0.223	1.777	0.975	3.078	0.223	1.777

$\text{UCL}_{\tilde{X}} + \text{LCL}_{\tilde{X}} = \bar{X} \pm A_2\bar{R}$
$\text{UCL}_{\bar{X}} = D_4\bar{R}$
$\text{LCL}_{\bar{X}} = D_3\bar{R}$
$\sigma = \bar{R}/d_2$

$\text{UCL}_{\bar{X}} + \text{LCL}_{\bar{X}} = \bar{X} \pm E_2\bar{R}$
$\text{UCL}_{\bar{X}} = D_4\bar{R}$
$\text{LCL}_{\bar{X}} = D_3\bar{R}$
$\sigma = \bar{R}/d_2$

*From ASTM publication STP–45D. *Manual on the Presentation of Data and Control Chart Analysis.* 1976: pp. 134–136. Copyright ASTM. 1916 Race Street, Philadelphia, Penn. 19103. Reprinted with permission.

**A factors derived from ASTM STP-15D data and efficiency tables contained in W. J. Dixon and F. J. Massey Jr. *Introduction to Statistical Analysis,* Third Edition. 1969: p. 488: McGraw-Hill Book Company, New York.

Figure D.9: Statistical Tables: Medial and Individual Charts

Assessment Tools

Continuous quality improvement survey	False	Rarely true	Sometimes true	Often true	Always true
1. My company has a continuous quality improvement strategy.	1 2 3 4 5				
2. Employees are involved in projects to improve the level of quality of our goods and services.	1 2 3 4 5				
3. Employees have received adequate training in performing their job functions.	1 2 3 4 5				
4. The company is committed to continuous education and training to ensure that employees are developed to their fullest potential.	1 2 3 4 5				
5. Primary and secondary processes in the company are well defined and documented.	1 2 3 4 5				
6. Primary and secondary processes in the company are capable of consistently producing the level of quality and productivity expected by the customer.	1 2 3 4 5				
7. Employees find their jobs rewarding both personally and professionally.	1 2 3 4 5				
8. The level of recognition for a job well done is adequate throughout the company.	1 2 3 4 5				
9. Reward structures within the company are consistent with the goals and objectives set by the management team.	1 2 3 4 5				
10. Customer feedback reveals that external customers are satisfied with the level of quality of our products and services.	1 2 3 4 5				
11. Feedback from internal customers is consistently used to judge individual and group performance.	1 2 3 4 5				
12. Employees have input to decision making that affects the quality, productivity, and performance of their work.	1 2 3 4 5				
13. Communication is open and effective in the company.	1 2 3 4 5				

Figure E.1: Assessment Survey

Continuous quality improvement survey	False	Rarely true	Sometimes true	Often true	Always true
14. Information is effectively and promptly passed through the levels of the company.	1	2	3	4	5
15. Communications between peer organizations and from management are effective.	1	2	3	4	5
16. Work groups and functional organizations work together effectively in teams.	1	2	3	4	5
17. The management team is consistent in its direction with respect to quality, productivity, and being customer and market driven.	1	2	3	4	5
18. Individuals and work groups are encouraged to seek new ways to serve the customer.	1	2	3	4	5
19. Key process measures are in place to steer the organization.	1	2	3	4	5
20. Employees are committed to improving quality, productivity, and customer satisfaction.	1	2	3	4	5

Figure E.1 (continued)

Bibliography

Amdsen, R. T. et al. *SPC Simplified Practical Steps to Quality*. White Plains, N.Y.: UniPub, 1986.

Argyris, C. *Intervening Theory and Method*. Reading, Mass.: Addison-Wesley Publishing, 1970.

Bennis, Warren, and Bert Nanus. *Leaders: The Strategies for Taking Charge*. New York: Harper & Row, 1985.

Bradford, D. L., and A. Cohen. *Managing for Excellence*. New York: John Wiley & Sons, 1984.

Bridges, William. *Surviving Corporate Transitions*. New York: Doubleday, 1989.

Buzzel, Robert D., Bradley T. Gale, and Ralph G. M. Sultan. "Market Share—Key to Profitability." *Harvard Business Review* (Jan.–Feb. 1975): 97–106.

Clemens, J. K. and D. F. Mayer. *The Classic Touch*. Homewood, Ill.: Dow Jones–Irwin, 1987.

Cohen, L. "Quality Function Deployment: An Application Perspective from Digital Equipment Corporation." *National Productivity Review* (Summer 1988): 197–208.

Crosby, Philip B. *Quality Is Free*. New York: The Free Press, 1979.

DeCarlo, N. J., and W. K. Sterett. "History of the Malcolm Baldrige National Quality Award." *Quality Progress*, March 1990, 29.

Deming, W. Edwards. *Quality, Productivity and Competitive Position*. Cambridge, Mass.: MIT Press, 1982.

———. *Out of the Crisis*. Cambridge, Mass.: MIT Press, 1986.

Dingus, V. R., and W. A. Golomski. *A Quality Revolution in Manufacturing*. Atlanta: Industrial Engineering and Management Press, 1988.

Drucker, Peter F. *Management*. New York: Harper & Row, 1974.

Duncan, A. J. *Quality Control and Industrial Statistics*. Homewood, Ill.: Richard D. Irwin, 1986.

Dyer, W. G. *Team Building: Issues and Alternatives*. Reading, Mass.: Addison-Wesley, 1977.

Edosowman, Johnson A. "Managing Technology in the Workplace: A Challenge for Industrial Engineers." *Industrial Engineering*, February 1986, 14–18.

———. "Technology Impact on the Quality of Working Life—A Challenge for Engineering Managers in the Year 2000." Arlington, Va.: Proceedings from the First International Conference on Engineering Management, 1986.

———. "Productivity and Quality Management—A Challenge in the Year 2000." Boston: Proceeding of Annual Industrial Engineering Conference, 1986.

———. *Integrating Productivity and Quality Management*. New York: Marcell Dekker, 1987.

———. "The Challenge for Industrial Managers: Productivity and Quality in the Workplace." *Industrial Management*, Sept./Oct. 1987, 24–27.

———. "Productivity and Quality Management: A Challenge for Industrial Manager. *Industrial Management*, Sept./Oct. 1987, 24–29.

———. "Perspective for Improving Managerial Performance." New York: IBM technical paper, 1987.

———. *Productivity and Quality Improvement*. Oxford, England: IFS Publications, 1988.

———. "A Practical Guide for Problem Solving and Completed Staff Work." New York: IBM technical report, 1989.

————. "Developing Market-Driven Leaders and Managers." IBM technical report, 1989.

————. "Continuous Improvement Through Problem Solving and Completed Staff Work." New York: IBM technical report, 1989.

————. "Excellence Through People." Atlanta: Institute of Industrial Engineers proceedings working paper, 1989.

————. "Improving the Quality of Management." New York: IBM technical report, 1989.

————. "Managing New Values in a High-Technology Environment." IBM technical paper, 1989.

————. "Preparing for Key Challenges and Changes in the '90s." Keynote speech, Institute of Industrial Engineers Spring conference, Chapter 32, Denver, Colo., 1989.

————. *Integrating Innovation and Technology Management*. New York: John Wiley & Sons, 1989.

————. "A Model for Improving Market-Driven Quality, Productivity, and Total Customer Satisfaction." Morgan Hill, Calif.: Johnson & Johnson Associates technical paper, 1990.

————. "Implementing Market-Driven Quality and Total Customer Satisfaction Programs." In *ASQC Annual Quality Congress Transactions*. Milwaukee, Wisc.: ASQC, 1990.

————. "Success Factors in Improving Total Quality in Manufacturing." Proceedings for the International Industrial Engineering Conference, San Francisco, 1990.

————. "Success Factors for Improving Quality, Productivity, Performance, and Total Customer Satisfaction." Atlanta: Industrial Engineering and Management Press, 1990.

————. *People and Product Management in Manufacturing*. Amsterdam, The Netherlands: Elsevier Science Publishers, 1990.

————. *Continuous Improvement Tools and Techniques*. Fairfax, Va.: Excellence Publications, 1991.

————. *Continuous Improvement Tools and Techniques Action Notebook*. Fairfax, Va.: Excellence Publications, Jan. 1991.

————. *The Winning Quality Manager*. Fairfax, Va.: Excellence Publications, June 1991.

————. "Baldrige National Quality Award: Focus on Total Customer Satisfaction." *Industrial Engineering*, 1991.

————. *Creating a Self-Directed Workforce*. Fairfax, Va.: Excellence Publications, 1991.

————. "Five Initiatives for Improving Your Customer Satisfaction Level." *The Quality Observer International News Magazine*, December 1991, 8.

————. *Understanding and Implementing Total Quality Management*. Fairfax, Va.: Excellence Publications, June 1991.

————. "On Becoming a Customer-Driven Organization." *The Quality Observer International News Magazine*, July 1991, 3.

————. "A Passion For Customer Satisfaction." *The Quality Observer International News Magazine*, February 1992, 7.

————. "Dealing with Customer Complaints." *The Quality Observer International News Magazine*, March 1992, 12.

Edosomwan, Johnson A., and Arvind Ballakar. *Productivity and Quality Improvement in Electronics Assembly*. New York: McGraw-Hill and Industrial Engineering and Management Press, 1988.

————. "ROI: How Long Before Quality Improvement Pays Off?" *Quality Progress*, Feb. 1987.

Feigenbaum, Armand V. *Total Quality Control*. New York: McGraw-Hill, 1983.

Fortuna, R. M. "Quality Function Deployment: Taking Quality Upstream." *TARGET*, Winter 1987, 11–16.

Gill, S. M. "Stalking Six Sigma." *Business Month*, January 1990, 37.

Goodman, H. F. "Improving Must Be Managed." *Industrial Engineering* 19, no. 11: 538–543.

Grant, Eugene L., and Richard S. Leavenworth. *Statistical Quality Control*. New York: McGraw-Hill, 1980.

Grocock, J. M. *The Chain of Quality*. New York: John Wiley & Sons, 1986.

Hacquebord, H. and P. R. Scholtes. *A Practical Approach to Quality*. Madison, Wis.: Joiner Associates, Inc., 1987.

Harrington, J. H. *Poor-Quality Costs*. New York and Milwaukee: Marcel Dekker and ASQC Quality Press, 1987.

————. *The Improvement Process.* New York: McGraw-Hill, 1987.

Harry, M. J. "The Nature of Six Sigma Quality." Schaumburg, Ill.: Motorola, Inc. Government Electronics Group Technical Paper, 1987.

Hauser, J. R., and D. Clausing. "The House of Quality." *Harvard Business Review* 66, no. 3 (May/June 1988): 63–73.

Hersey, P., and K. H. Blanchard. *Management of Organizational Behavior: Utilizing Human Resources.* Englewood Cliffs, N.J.: Prentice-Hall, 1977.

Imai, Masaaki. *Kaizen.* New York: Random House, 1986.

Ishikawa, Kaoru. *Guide to Quality Control.* Tokyo: Asian Productivity Organization, 1976.

————. "What Is Total Quality Control?" *The Japanese Way.* Englewood Cliffs, N.J.: Prentice-Hall, 1985.

Juran, J. M. *Managerial Breakthrough.* New York: McGraw-Hill, 1964.

————. *Quality Control Handbook.* New York: McGraw-Hill, 1979.

————. *Quality Planning and Analysis.* New York: McGraw-Hill, 1979.

————. "Product Quality—A Presentation for the West." *Management Review,* June/July 1981, 16.

————. "The Quality Trilogy." *Quality Progress,* August 1986, 19–24.

Kanter, Rosabeth M. *Men and Women of the Corporation.* New York: Basic Books, 1977.

————. *The Change Masters: Innovations for Productivity in American Corporations.* New York: Simon & Schuster, 1983.

————. "Managing the Human Side of Change." *Management Review,* April 1985.

King, B. "Listening to the Voice of the Customer: Using the Quality Function Deployment System." *National Productivity Review,* Summer 1987, 277–281.

Kogure, M., and Y. Akao. "Quality Function Deployment and Company-Wide Quality Control in Japan." *Quality Progress,* October 1983, 25–29.

Kotler, Philip. "From Sales Obsession to Marketing Effectiveness." *Harvard Business Review,* Nov./Dec. 1977.

————. "Marketization: *The Art of Creating Market-Driven Businesses.*" Chicago: Northwestern University, 1989.

Kouzes, J. M., and B. Posner. *The Leadership Challenge.* San Francisco: Jossey-Bass, 1987.

Lefevre, H. L. *Quality Service Pays.* Milwaukee: ASQC Quality Press, 1989.

Levinson, H., and S. Rosenthal. *CEO: Corporate Leadership in Action.* New York: Basic Books, 1984.

Maccoby, M. *The Leader.* New York: Simon & Schuster, 1981.

Moen, Ronald D., and Thomas W. Nolan. "Process Improvement." *Quality Progress,* September 1987, 62–68.

Peters, T., and N. Austin. *A Passion for Excellence: The Leadership Difference.* New York: Random House, 1985.

Peters, T., and R. H. Waterman, Jr. *In Search of Excellence.* New York: Harper & Row, 1982.

Porter, Michael E. *Competitive Strategy.* New York: The Free Press, 1980.

Reilly, A. J., and J. E. Jones, *Handbook for Group Facilitators.* San Diego: University Associates, 1974.

Reimann, C. W. "The Baldrige Award: Leading the Way in Quality Initiatives." *Quality Progress,* July 1989.

Re Velle, J. B. *The New Quality Technology: An Introduction to Quality Function Deployment and the Taguchi Methods.* Los Angeles: Hughes Aircraft, 1988.

Rosander, A. C. *The Quest for Quality in Services.* Milwaukee: ASQC Quality Press, 1989.

Rummler, Gary A., and Alan P. Brache. *How to Manage the White Space on the Organizational Chart.* San Francisco: Jossey-Bass, 1990.

Sayles, L. R. *Leadership: What Effective Managers Really Do and How They Do It.* New York: McGraw-Hill, 1979.

Schein, E. H. *Organizational Culture and Leadership: A Dynamic View.* San Francisco: Jossey-Bass, 1985.

Scherkenbach, William. *The Deming Route to Quality and Productivity.* Washington, D.C.: Ceepress, 1986.

Schneiderman, A. M. "Quality Optimum Costs and Zero Defects: Are They Contradictory Concepts?" *Quality Progress*, June 1986, 28–31.

Scholtes, P. R. "A Practical Approach to Quality." Madison, Wis.: Joiner Associates, Inc., 1987.

Scholtes, P. R. et. al. *The Team Handbook: How to Use Teams to Improve Quality*. Madison, Wis.: Joiner Associates, 1988.

Schonberger, Richard J. *Japanese Manufacturing Techniques: Nine Hidden Lessons in Simplicity*. New York: The Free press, 1982.

Scott, D. Cynthia, and T. Dennis Jaffe. *Managing Organizational Change*. Los Altos, Calif.: Crisp Publications, 1989.

Shewhart, Walter A. *The Economic Control of Quality of Manufactured Product*. Milwaukee: ASQC Quality Press, 1980.

Skinner, Wickham. "Operations Technology: Blind Spot in Strategic Management." *Interfaces* 14 (Jan./Feb. 1984):

Sullivan, L. P. "Policy Deployment Through Quality Function Deployment." *Quality Progress* 21 (June 1988): 18–20.

Sumanth, D. J. *Productivity Engineering and Management*. New York: McGraw-Hill, 1984.

Tichy, N., and D. Ulrich. "The Leadership Challenge—A Call for the Transformational Leader." *Sloan Management Review*, Fall 1984, 59–68.

Torbert, William. *Managing the Corporate Dream*. Homewood, Ill.: Dow Jones Irwin, 1986.

Townsend, Patrick L. *Commit to Quality*. New York: John Wiley & Sons, 1986.

Webster, Frederick, Jr., "Top Management's Concerns About Marketing: Issues for the 1980s." *Journal of Marketing*, Summer 1981, 9–16.

———. "Rediscovering the Marketing Concept." Cambridge, Mass.: Marketing Science Institute, Report No. 88–100, 1988.

Wheeler, D. J., and D. S. Chambers. *Understanding Statistical Process Control*. Knoxville, Tenn.: Statistical Process Controls, 1986.

Index